Teaching Design and Technology 3 – 11

Biographical note

Douglas Newton taught in schools for more than two decades before training teachers at Newcastle University where he is a professor. He is an inventor himself and has written several very successful books on science and technology education and has received awards for his work. He is also a Professional Fellow at Durham University where he contributes to the science and technology training of undergraduate and postgraduate trainee teachers. His research is largely to do with strategies that support understanding, particularly in connection with learning science and technology. Professor Newton's numerous publications have attracted a worldwide readership and have been translated into other languages.

Teaching Design and Technology 3–11

Douglas Newton

P·C·P

Paul Chapman Publishing

Paul Chapman Publishing
A SAGE Publications Company
1 Oliver's Yard
55 City Road
London EC1Y 1SP

SAGE Publications Inc.
2455 Teller Road
Thousand Oaks, California 91320

SAGE Publications India Pvt Ltd
B-42, Panchsheel Enclave
Post Box 4109
New Delhi 110 017

Library of Congress Control Number: 2004114473

A catalogue record for this book is available from the British Library

ISBN 1 4129 0160 X
ISBN 1 4129 0161 8 (pbk)

Typeset by Pantek Arts Ltd, Maidstone, Kent
Printed in Great Britain by Athenaeum Press, Gateshead

Contents

Foreword

Since the publication of *Design and Technology 5 to 12* by Williams and Jinks in 1985, there have been hundreds of books written about Design and Technology in primary schools. I have read a considerable number of these books and they range from the very ordinary to those of high quality. Doug Newton's book fits into the latter category.

From the opening chapter, where Doug looks at Design and Technology from a practical problem-solving point of view, through his description of designing and making as a 'rather erratic and messy process involving false starts', Doug displays a clear understanding of this most fascinating subject. His comment in the final chapter that 'D&T can benefit from a guardian and a champion, someone showing diplomacy, forethought and the skills of persuasion' demonstrates his clear, sympathetic under-standing of a subject still trying to establish a secure place in the primary school curriculum. This book is packed full of sound advice and good ideas interlaced with the essence of what Design and Technology in primary schools should be. The middle chapters provide a plethora of imaginative design and make activities for children across the age range 3 – 11; they are divided into the age bands 3 – 5, 5 – 7, and 7 – 11. It is difficult to bring to mind other publications that offer more opportunities across a range of starting points covering materials appropriate to the age of the children.

Whether you are a student working your way through an initial teacher training course, recently qualified facing the onerous task of delivering the subjects of the National Curriculum or a seasoned primary school practitioner, this book will be a most welcome addition to your list of curriculum subject favourites. I wish Doug suc-cess with his book and all primary school teachers success in their classrooms.

David Jinks
Jerwood Laureate for contributions to
Design and Technology Education

Preface

A concern for technology teaching and for the plight of teachers (trainee, newly-qualified and experienced) working with children between 3 and 11 years of age has led to this book. It is a practical book which gives you what you need so you can fit in with the teaching in your school. I have avoided approaches that would make your teaching abnormal or eccentric and I have omitted esoteric debate that tells us little about the practicalities of the classroom. I see this as essential for hard pressed trainees and it is no less important for newly-qualified teachers who may have had no more than a taste of training in technology teaching, if that. The need to develop skills in this area is likely to figure in their plans for professional development. More experienced teachers will find the book useful both as a source of ideas and to add to their thoughts about what technology education can be about.

Technology makes Western life what it is. Love it or hate it, that is reality. People have no urgent wish to put on home-cured skins, boil pots of gruel over open fires or cauterize wounds in the kitchen with hot pokers. They generally prefer technology's convenience, comfort and help. Children meet this technological world even as they are born and should be prepared for an adult life in it, prepared to make the most of what is good about it and prepared to reject what is not. This is not a matter of telling them what is good and bad. In the real world, few things are black or white and, even if they were, technology changes so children must be equipped to make up their own minds. Growing up with technology tends to make them take it for granted. Being taught Design and Technology can open children's eyes to it and begin to develop their critical faculties. At the same time, it can help dispel stereotyped thinking. Images of activities that are 'right' for men and 'wrong' for women and 'right' for women and 'wrong' for men begin to develop very early, even in five and six year olds. They can be well-established and hard to change once children reach the secondary school. An early start gives you a chance to help children widen their horizons and realize their potential, instead of denying themselves opportunities on irrational grounds.

But technology has still more to offer. In England, for instance, the *National Primary Strategy: Excellence and Enjoyment* (2003), expresses the concern that children should have significant opportunities to be creative. Design and Technology can make a major contribution to those opportunities as it is about solving practical problems, an activity that exercises creativity. Amongst the school subjects, few can make such a clear and unambiguous claim and to ignore the creativity involved in practical problem-solving would be to neglect a dimension that is within the grasp of most of us. This kind of creativity has a direct relevance to the everyday life of the child and the adult. It may help to foster an independence of thought and action that helps children make the most of their abilities and avoid exploitation and manipulation.

Given what technology has to offer, it is disappointing to find that it can be neglected. For instance, when schools find that they must give more time elsewhere, as to literacy and numeracy, technology tends to have time whittled from it and is pushed into a corner of the curriculum. Even science, a subject that can underpin much activity in technology, can suffer in this way. At the same time, although primary school teachers have to teach technology, it is astonishing that it can be optional in their training. Inevitably, many training institutions offer only a 'taster' course amounting to a day or two of instruction, if that. Books like this may be the only kind of training some teachers receive in this aspect of the curriculum. I hope it helps.

A note on safety

You must ensure that the activities you provide for children are safe and comply with national and local regulations and recommendations. You must assess for yourself any risks associated with activities taking into account the children's attributes, the materials, the equipment and the context and then act appropriately. The author and publisher do not accept responsibility for this nor for any loss (however caused) arising from the practice of any suggestions, procedures or activities described in this book.

CHAPTER 1

What is Design and Technology?

Just the words Design and Technology (D&T) make some people nervous. What comes to mind are enormous machines in factories, personal computers, helicopters, holograms, photocopiers, robots, space stations, mobile telephones and televisions. But we tend to overlook the enormous number of familiar things we have around us that are neither complicated nor expensive: brooms, forks, egg whisks, pencils, erasers, sticking plasters, torches, toys, paper weights, mitts, mixed fruit drinks, buttons, teabags, rubber boots, safety rulers, spinning top: no book is long enough to list them all. Children can understand things like these. What is more, they can design and make simple things like these themselves and solve practical problems with a small number of tools and materials. D&T need not be complex and doing D&T does not have to involve rolls of blueprints or machines. So, what is it?

Inventions that solve practical problems

Design and Technology is the process of inventing or improving things to satisfy practical needs and solve practical problems. Think of a ball of wool in a shop window. The shopkeeper wants to attach a price tag. The problem is that some ways of attaching a tag could damage the wool. Then no one would buy it – think of those annoying holes that some tags make in garments. But, if the tag is not attached firmly, it could drop off. What is the solution? One solution is to cut out a rather broad, blunt arrow-head from thin card. The 'pointed' end is pushed into the ball of wool and the price is written on the piece that sticks out. Being V-shaped, the card does not fall out and, made from thin card, it does not damage the wool. This is just one solution and you could probably think of others. Simple practical problems like these that can be solved in many different ways are very useful in the classroom. They give the children the opportunity to be creative and solve the problems in their own way.

Here is another practical problem. Think about a pile of loose sheets of paper on your desk. Someone walks past and the papers fall to the floor and become mixed-up. How can you prevent that happening? You might, for instance, put the sheets in order and push a pin through one corner. This was how papers used to be attached to letters and, of course, you would probably catch a finger on the pin as you took the letter from the envelope. The pin is a solution, but not an ideal one. Something

1

cheap that can hold a few pages together without injuring those who handle them is needed. The improvement is, of course, the wire paper clip, invented by the Norwegian, Johan Vaaler in 1899.

Ideas can come from anywhere. Temporary fasteners for items of clothing are an obvious need and the button and the zip are two solutions. In the 1950s, George de Mestral was walking in the countryside in Switzerland and noticed that burdock seed heads – burrs – clung to his clothes. A microscope showed him how they did it. Each spine ended in a tiny hook. This hook solves the problem of seed dispersal for the plant but de Mestral went on to use it to make another solution to the problem of fastening clothes, Velcro®. This has tiny plastic hooks on a strip of fabric. Another strip has tiny loops. When the two are pressed together, hooks and loops engage and keep the strips together.

Often, inventions do not solve a new problem but improve upon an existing solution. Take clothes-pegs, for example. Originally, these were split twigs bound at one end, but after a while, the binding becomes loose. An improvement was to make a one-piece wooden peg, but these have a tendency to split so there was still room for improvement. The next step was a peg with two wooden legs held together by a spring. After that, the wood was replaced by a plastic material. This peg would not split but it is still not perfect. Sunlight and use weaken plastic pegs and they tend to snap. New designs for clothes-pegs continue to appear.

Inventions in history and everywhere

Inventing things to solve practical problems or make things work better is not something new. People have done it for thousands of years. Remarkable evidence of this comes from the frozen, 5000 year old remains of a man found in the mountains on the Austrian–Italian border. He was wearing a fur cap, a cape and leggings. Around his waist was a belt with a pouch to hold his fire-making materials. His leather shoes were lined with hay to keep his feet warm and he wore a cloak made from grass over his clothes to shed rain like a thatched roof. He had a flint knife in a plaited sheath, a bow and some arrows and, like a modern hill-walker, a backpack. He even carried a medicine kit containing a fungus that could be used to deal with infected wounds. These are solutions to some of the most fundamental problems we all face: keeping dry and warm, collecting and preparing food, carrying things and keeping healthy. Amusement and entertainment, though not essential for survival, are also needs that people seek to satisfy. It was no different long ago. For instance, a toy crocodile made from wood was found in an ancient Egyptian child's tomb. Its lower jaw was held in place by a simple hinge and when a string was pulled, the jaw would snap shut. We can easily imagine this child pestering her brothers and sisters with her snappy crocodile, just like a modern child would do. In China, at much the same time, people were playing flutes made from hollow bones and in the Middle East, they were making lute-like instruments using natural fibres for the strings.

All people face practical problems and try to solve them, no matter when or where they live. For example, enormous waterwheels were constructed in India centuries ago. They were used to irrigate fields by lifting water from rivers. The Greeks and Egyptians constructed water clocks because sun dials do not work at night and cannot indicate small intervals of time clearly. The Chinese made a clever earthquake detector that rocked to and fro in response to a tremor. The motion made balls fall into the mouths of metal frogs. Nor is ingenuity confined to adults; children all over the world use what is to hand to make their toys.

Inventors: men and women

Customs, past divisions of labour and the way history is written can give the impression that inventing is something done mainly by men. This is not the case and probably never was. Men and women solve problems in whatever they do. For instance, if your life is centred on domestic affairs, you will tend to meet domestic problems. In 1893, Josephine Cochran invented the dishwasher. Presumably, she saw the tiresome drudgery of washing dishes by hand. In 1904, Annie England patented a spoon that would hook over a treacle-tin so that it dripped into the tin, rather than made a mess on the table. Perhaps she had had enough of mopping up sticky treacle when using a conventional spoon. In the same year, Sophia Turner patented an ear-flattener. When asleep, children may lie on their ears in a way that makes them stick out. The ear-flattener was intended to prevent this. Presumably, she had noticed the problem when caring for children and set out to solve it. A more noisome problem is that of washing nappies. Whoever deals with that soon wants an improvement and in 1951, Marion Donovan invented the disposable nappy. Such concerns arose from domestic problems. When your concerns are elsewhere, so is your inventiveness. For instance, in 1870, Margaret Knight, a shop assistant in Boston, invented a satchel-bottomed paper bag, still used today. Presumably, she saw the need and how such bags would make life easier.

At about that time, Stanley Webb, a butcher, patented 'Webb's Improved Skewer'. Being a butcher, he would need something to display the price of his products. His solution was a thick wire spike with a curly top to hold the price ticket. Men have a problem with the daily growth of beard hair. For many years, the solution was to scrape off the hair with a 'cut-throat' razor, an implement which is hard to use, hard to keep sharp, and scary. K.C. Gillette solved the problem in a better way, with the disposable razor blade fitted into his safety razor. If you spend a lot of your time dealing with paper, your problems will often be paper-related. There will have been times when you had a mug in one hand, a biscuit in the other and found you needed a third hand for your papers. Dominic Skinner recently solved that problem by making a mug with a biscuit shelf so you need only one hand for your coffee and biscuit.

The point is that the situation makes the need. Sooner or later, someone will have a go at solving the problem or satisfying the need. If women had beards,

K.C. Gillette might have been a woman. If Stanley Webb had worked with treacle, he might have invented the hooked spoon. If Margaret Knight had worked in Webb's shop, she might have invented the price ticket skewer. If men had been the ones to wash nappies, it could have been a man who invented the disposable nappy. The practical problems you meet are determined by your situation. Change it and you meet different problems, some of which you may solve.

This is not to say, however, that boys and girls do not develop their own interests and ways of responding to the tasks you set. These can even support what you are trying to achieve. For instance, some girls may care enormously about the appearance of their design plans. As a consequence, the drawing and written work they hand in can look good. But take care not to think in stereotypes. Do not assume that all girls are like this or that no boys are like this.

Solving practical problems can also be the concern of businesses. They look for opportunities and seek to make a product that satisfies a need (or desire) and fills a vacant niche in the market. So, for instance, we have washing machines for the household market, electric hand drills for the DIY market, paving blocks for the building industry and self-service restaurants at motorway stops.

But invention and innovation are not the exclusive preserves of large companies. Mary Phelps Jacob, prompted by the appearance of her corset under her gown, invented a 'backless brassiere' in 1913 and sold the idea to a corset company. Ladislao Biro, working independently, invented the ballpoint pen in the 1930s. Working as a secretary, Bette Graham saw the need for a paint to cover typing errors so she invented Liquid Paper then, in the 1950s, manufactured it herself, eventually selling the business to a larger company. More recently, James Dyson spent years working alone on his 'cyclone' vacuum cleaner before it appeared on the market. At the same time, the products people create are not always devices that you pick up and use in the conventional sense of the term. Arthur Wynne, for instance, was a journalist who had the problem of providing something to entertain people in the 1913 Christmas issue of his paper. His solution was the crossword puzzle.

Not all inventions are successful or serious but inventing them can be fun

Inevitably, we are surrounded by inventions that are successful. Think of the sweeping brush, the eraser, pens and pencils, bed springs, and the mass of other items we often take for granted. Those that do not make it just disappear. Some years ago, Clive Sinclair invented the C5, an open-topped buggy for getting around town. It used a battery-powered washing machine motor to propel a lightweight body big enough for one. On the surface, this affordable, electrically-propelled buggy sounds like a good idea yet very few people bought it. Compared with the conventional car, it could not compete so that was the end of it. The patent records are full of ideas that never made it. Children, however, do not know of these and so have a distorted image of invention. They may think that all inventions are good and make it onto the market.

In Japan, there is the Art of Chindogu. A Chindogu is an invention that solves a problem but it is more effort than it is worth or creates another problem or is simply not something we would want to do. For example, if a baby has reached the crawling stage, why not put him or her to good use as a mop? Sew mop heads onto her romper suits and set her free on the floor. Why struggle with an umbrella? Fit one to your hat. Never burn your tongue again. Use a plastic tongue-cover. A Chindogu is an invention that simply amuses you. Inventing can be a lot of fun.

D&T and children

What does D&T have to offer children? First, the made world is a very significant part of life for most children and adults. Through D&T, children can begin to understand the made world and have well-founded confidence in dealing with issues in it. They can, for instance, think about what makes a good product, choose wisely from competing products and begin to learn what influences designing and making. Second, learning to solve practical problems benefits from practice and guidance. In D&T, the child can learn to handle ill-defined problems that have many acceptable solutions. People with this capability have a certain kind of independence and autonomy. Third, D&T gives opportunities to acquire or supplement various life skills, such as working co-operatively and communicating effectively. Fourth, because D&T can draw on knowledge from any area of experience, it can serve a useful function in tying knowledge together for the children, making it more concrete and meaningful and memorable. Fifth, learning about D&T and engaging in it prepares the way for further learning and, in the longer term, employment for some. But children cannot acquire all of this at once. It has to be staged.

The 3 – 5 stage

An early stage relates to children between 3 and 5 years of age. This tends to be referred to as the early years, pre-school, or foundation stage. In practice, this stage overlaps with the period of compulsory schooling in the UK so that it includes   children in the reception or first class of the primary school. There are various guidelines for practice in this stage. For instance, in England, these organize the curriculum into six 'learning areas': personal, social and emotional development; communication, language and literacy; mathematical development; knowledge and understanding of the world; physical development and creative development. In Wales, the areas are similar with the addition of bilingual and multicultural understanding. In Scotland, expressive and aesthetic development is included while in Northern Ireland, 'early experiences in Science and Technology' is a specific inclusion. Broadly speaking, these curricula are not subject-centred but prepare the children for what they will do later. For consistency, this stage will be referred to as *the early years stage* or by reference to the age range it encompasses (*3 – 5 stage*). The children in it will be decribed as *very young children* if describing them otherwise would be ambiguous.

D&T-like activities can make a useful contribution to any of the learning areas of the early years stage. It can, for instance, help the very young child acquire new ways of working and confidence in working independently and with others (as when using scissors to cut out shapes for a greetings card and sharing them with others). It can provide opportunities to explore, predict and experience the satisfaction and pleasure of simple problem-solving and making activities (as when finding a way to help Winnie the Pooh move a large box). It can provide opportunities to describe, explain, discuss and use pictures for ideas to support their thinking (as when choosing an animal to make). There are opportunities for learning ways of doing things, like how to make copies of the same shape (as when making ladybird 'wings' from card), counting, and measuring by comparison. Both through the contexts used and what is made, children can add to their knowledge and understanding (as when they find that ladybirds have six legs and are harmless to people). Practical activities are opportunities for very young children to increase their planning and manipulative skills and hand-eye co-ordination (as when making a tail that will wag for a shoe box dog and the children have to work inside and outside the box at the same time). Open parts of activities give children the opportunity to make decisions and try out their ideas (as when deciding what the picture on a greetings card will be).

The 5–7 stage

The next stage applies to children between 5 and 7 years of age. These are firmly in the period of compulsory schooling. In England and Wales, these children in state schools are subject to the Key Stage 1 requirements of the National Curriculum, of which Design and Technology is one subject. (In Wales, by 2008 the term, 'Foundation Phase', will describe the period 3 – 7 years of age and a revised curriculum will apply). The requirements in Northern Ireland and the National Guidelines for Scotland include technology as an aspect of The World Around Us and Environmental Studies, respectively. This period of schooling will be referred to as the *5 – 7 stage*. The children in it will be decribed as *younger children* if describing them otherwise would be ambiguous.

How the children's day is organized is for the school to decide but, even where subjects are specified, this does not mean that younger children will have subject-centred lessons. A single, interesting topic may be used to achieve goals in a variety of subjects. Often, a topic will provide a meaningful context for D&T and younger children may not notice the move from one subject to another.

The exercise and development of thinking skills is also generally expected in the 5 – 7 stage. These include:

- information-processing skills (D&T can contribute here when, for instance, you have children search through pictures of playgrounds to find a range of play equipment to model);

- reasoning skills (as when you ask children to explain how a given toy works);

- enquiry skills (as when children test their ideas for how they will make a tall, thin vase stand up even when it has very large flowers in it),

- creative thinking skills (as when, for instance, children have a bright idea about how to make a model roundabout turn, or turn better, or work with fewer parts or how to make it look good);

- evaluation skills (as when you ask the children how the wheels performed on their buggies and how they might do things differently next time).

Practical problem-solving can practise these and more and some curricula list problem-solving as a skill in itself.

Other aspects of learning that are expected include financial capability, enterprise education and education for sustainable development. There are times when D&T activities can contribute to these (as when you have children 'buy' the materials they need using a fixed amount of money in the form of plastic coins and when you take opportunities to have children solve practical problems to do with avoiding waste and caring for their environment).

The 7 – 11 stage

The next stage is for 7 – 11 year olds. In England, Wales and Northern Ireland, this is commonly referred to as Key Stage 2 in state schools. Again, communication, number, co-operative working and problem-solving are to be developed across the curriculum and D&T teaching is required in England and Wales. As in the earlier stage, technology features in The World Around Us and in Environmental Studies in Northern Ireland and Scotland, respectively. This stage will be referred to as the *7 – 11 stage*. The children in it will be decribed as *older children* if describing them otherwise would be ambiguous.

This is a long stage and, to begin with, many of the children can be quite like those in the earlier stage. They affiliate readily with you and look to you for affirmation and support. As yet, their skills are often unrefined. Because they lack well-digested experience, practical problems can be difficult to understand. The oldest children in this stage, however, are often more skilled. They know more of the world and of D&T and can address more open problems. They may also tend to look more to their peers for affiliation, affirmation and support. Between 7 and 11 years of age, an increasing emphasis is often placed on the teaching of distinct subjects. Contexts for D&T, however, often arise in other areas of the curriculum. Taking these opportunities can make D&T meaningful for the children. Just as important is what it can do for learning. It can develop and integrate children's knowledge and make it more durable. Science will often inform and lead into D&T activities and a practical problem in D&T can lead to an investigation in science. Take advantage of this symbiotic relationship and of those everyday events that point to a need or problem to solve. As you are also expected to foster problem-solving skills, D&T has a significant role to play in helping you do that. You are also expected to foster creativity. Again, D&T provides opportunities for that as children search for novel solutions.

As before, the development of thinking skills is expected. In this stage, this can mean:

- information-processing skills (as when children produce a guide book using ICT to find information and when they use a programmable switch to operate traffic lights);

- reasoning skills (when you ask children to explain why a particular bridge fell down);

- enquiry skills (when children investigate how much cannot be seen from a car driver's seat);

- creative thinking skills (when you ask the children for ideas for making a buggy's wheels turn without using a motor or elastic band);

- evaluation skills (when you have the children try out their model land yachts in a breeze and comment on design improvements).

In these three stages, D&T provides opportunities to develop certain useful tendencies and skills. These include:

- an inclination to generate ideas;

- an inclination to suggest ways of doing things;

- an inclination to consider alternatives;

- an inclination to plan ahead;

- an inclination to select appropriate tools;

- the skill to mark out shapes (for example, using a template, using a ruler, using compasses);

- the skill to shape materials (for example, by folding, tearing, crushing, rolling; moulding, cutting using safe tools along lines, using pastry cutters);

- the skill to join or combine materials (for example, using adhesive tape, safe glue; stapling, paper clips and fasteners, treasury tags, sewing, nailing, pegging);

- an inclination to assemble loosely or model some part of what they will make in paper or card to check it works as expected;

- an inclination to consider matters of hygiene and safety of self and others, unprompted;

- an inclination to seek out information or investigate to find the information, as needed;

- an inclination to consider the appearance of products and to finish them well (for example, by applying colour, fabrics, glitter, sand, water-based paint, wax polish, PVA glue as a glaze);

- an ability to describe and explain what they are doing;

- an ability to demonstrate what they will do or have done;

- the skill to test products in simple ways;

- the skill to work with others and help others.

Of course, some of these will develop before others.
   Children may develop these tendencies and skills working with materials such as:

- papers of various kinds;

- card (strictly speaking, a kind of paper);

- cooking foil;

- flexible plastic sheet;

- reclaimed materials (for example, card tubes from the kitchen, card boxes);

- foodstuffs;

- fabrics/textiles;

- wood;

- clay and similar modelling materials;

- simple construction kits;

- electrical components and electronic devices.

How these are used will, of course, depend on the stage and skills of the child.

D&T and science

Some say that D&T is the appliance of science. Science produces knowledge and understanding of the world. At times, this can be very useful as when we use our knowledge of electrical circuits to help us construct a model lighthouse or use the fact that a hollow box can amplify sound when making a musical instrument, or that a lever can magnify movement to make a card rabbit pop up. But you will need to remember that just because you have 'done it' in science, it does not follow that the children will be able to use it in D&T. For example, circuits neatly set out in science using a kit are one thing; making your own circuit from a roll of plastic-covered wire, a bulb without a holder, and a battery without clips to keep the wires in place is another. In the same way, translating the tests you did on a strip of wood balanced over a pencil like a see-saw into something that will make a cardboard rabbit pop up out of a hole, is another. Bridging the know-how gap becomes a problem in itself. The children are likely to need your help in bridging from science knowledge to what is sometimes called 'device' knowledge. When successful, however, the benefits are enormous because what you taught in science becomes more meaningful and memorable.

At times, you can bring science and D&T close together. For instance, suppose you set the children the challenge of building a bridge from paper that would be strong enough to take a certain toy car. Which shapes are likely to be the strongest ones they could use to support the bridge? In science, the children make tubes of various cross-sections and test them. They then immediately use what they find in their D&T. Solving a problem in science (Which shapes are the strongest?) provides the knowledge to be applied to solve a problem in D&T (How do I make a bridge strong enough to take that toy car?).

Just as D&T is not Science, D&T is not Art or Craft. Art is about expression and aesthetics. D&T may draw on Art skills because we want things to be functional and look, feel or sound good. At times, however, it may be hard to distinguish between D&T and Art. For example, if you had to design and make a wrapper for a new, chewy, dried fruit bar, would it be Art or D&T? You have to ask why the wrapper was needed. Is it to solve a practical problem? A dried fruit bar probably needs a wrapper for the sake of hygiene but the manufacturer would also want people to recognize the product from its wrapper and that is a practical problem solved, in part, by drawing on artistic knowledge and skills. That makes it D&T. Of course, the expression and beauty of the wrapper may make it a collector's piece and like Toulouse Lautrec's posters, an object of art. If that was also your intention, then it is also Art.

Craft is about developing practical skills. D&T involves craft skills but is more than these alone. You may, for instance, develop craft skills by following instructions or a recipe or by copying the actions of an expert. But this does not mean you exercise your imagination to create a design for a new product. That should happen in D&T.

D&T and ability

Problem-solving is generally seen as exercising higher level thinking. As such, how can it be suitable for all children? The experience of designing and making is a valuable one but it is worse than pointless to give children tasks that are beyond them. How is D&T to be made accessible to all?

Most of the challenges or problems we set the children are open to a variety of solutions. Take, for instance, the flashing lighthouse problem. The light can be made to flash by repeatedly pressing one of the wires onto the battery terminal. It could be made to flash by constructing a switch and pressing it repeatedly. Alternatively, cooking foil could be used to make a 'comb' with a pattern to its teeth so that, when a wire is dragged over it, the light flashes according to that pattern. And it could be made to flash using a ready-made box of electronics. Such a task lends itself to solutions with different degrees of complexity and demand. There is a level for just about everyone.

Problems also have various levels of openness. For example, 'Design and make something that will help ships know where they are and avoid rocks', is more open than 'Design and make a model lighthouse with a flashing light'. The former is less focused on a particular solution. This adds to the demand because the child has to grasp the general problem and explore what it means in order to solve it. Of course, in the process, the child's solution may not be a lighthouse. You can present a problem at different levels to tune the demand to the child's abilities. Nevertheless, at times you will have to support some children more than others and help them develop their thinking and doing. You may, for instance, point the way to a solution. For example, suppose you draw the children's attention to the way everyone seems to trip over the doormat. You might ask, 'How can we warn people about the doormat?'. This directs thoughts to warning signs. For others, you might ask, 'What can we do about it?'. This directs thoughts towards doing something to repair the mat. Do not forget, however, that the aim is to help children make progress. Always keep them working at a level that is sufficiently challenging to exercise thought and action in more proficient and complex ways, whatever their abilities.

Summary

This chapter has described Design and Technology from a practical problem-solving point of view. People have always invented solutions to such problems, wherever and whenever they lived. The problems we tend to think about are those around us. Put us in a different context and we will notice different problems and respond to them. Stereotypes can develop when men and women are assigned to different contexts. Care is needed to ensure that children see these stereotypes for what they are. Working with wood is not just for boys and working with food and textiles is not just for girls. D&T has a lot to offer the primary school child, not least being how to manage thought and action in more or less ill-defined situations. D&T can be a demanding subject but it can also be motivating and accommodating. Nevertheless, you will need to think about what you will do to ensure that all children make the most of the learning opportunities it offers.

CHAPTER 2

Thoughtful Designing and Making

D&T in action

Amongst other things, designing involves coming up with and shaping ideas. Making is about turning those ideas into reality. This sounds like two, distinct steps: first, design; second, make. Life is not so simple. In practice, we may have an idea, get a feel for a part of it, try it and adapt or change the idea, make sure it does what we want, in the process find something we had not thought of, adjust the idea to take that into account and, to cut the story short, we (eventually) arrive at a product. In other words, designing and making can be a messy business with some making while we are designing and some designing while we are making. Figure 2.1 summarizes the way designing and making interact. While things to do with designing dominate in the early stages, they do not entirely disappear, even in the later stages. Similarly, things to do with making can appear early.

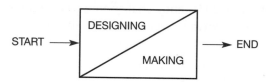

Figure 2.1 *There is often interplay between designing and making as a task progresses.*

This is not to say, however, that designing and making are chaotic, haphazard processes, amounting to nothing more than blind fumblings which sometimes produce something useful. Designing and making are meant to be thoughtful processes that inform one another. Nevertheless, presenting them separately simplifies explanation.

Designing

Designing is the process of generating and developing ideas that seem likely to solve a practical problem or satisfy some practical need. Of course, ideas have to be turned into products before we can be sure a problem has been solved so having and developing ideas alone is not enough.

Designing is not like, say, long division. In long division, you follow the rules and are generally guaranteed the right answer. It is better to think of designing as a journey. But this is a journey that could lead to several different places, all acceptable. In addition, the map you have is rather vague. There are many ways of getting to these places and you are not certain of any of them. You may have been puzzled by the title of this chapter. Surely, there can be no such thing as thoughtless designing. This is true but some designing journeys are more thoughtful than others. Do you approach the journey in a systematic way, choosing a promising route or simply wait to see what others are doing and follow them? When asked why you chose that route, can you give a good reason? Do you actively watch the scenary looking for alternatives or do you follow the road passively and let it take you where it will, even when there is not the faintest hint of the journey's end on the horizon? Do you ever decide that your mode of transport is not up to it and change to something more promising, or do you let it take you on until it breaks down?

Without taking the analogy too far, designing is like such a journey. It is not casting about in a random way in the hope of finding something that will do the trick. The design process is shaped by reason. Your actions are chosen because you have good reason to believe that they will lead towards a solution. At times, however, 'good reason' leads you astray and you go down a blind alley. But good reason helps you recognize that and backtrack or make a fresh start. If a particular course of action lacks promise, good reason helps you choose another. In other words, as you design, you judge the results as you go along. You respond to that judgement, adapting or changing to what you have reason to believe is a promising course of action. Allowing for age and experience, the goal is to help the children move towards this way of working.

The mousetrap

Here is a designing journey. Think of the conventional mousetrap. To many people, this is an effective but repugnant device, particularly when they catch a field mouse that only came in to get out of the winter cold. Many would prefer a non-lethal trap that would catch a mouse so it could be released outside. To illustrate the skills involved, have a go at designing such a mousetrap for yourself. Ask yourself, 'What exactly is needed?'. and 'How will I know if I succeed?'. When you have a couple of ideas, choose the one that you think is most promising. Ask yourself, 'Why did I choose it? What makes it most promising?'. Now take a sheet of paper and develop the idea in more detail with a drawing (it does not have to be a work of art). Ask yourself, 'How exactly will this bit work?' 'What might go wrong?' 'How could I prevent that?' 'Does it look good?' 'How could I make it look better?'. Now, in the process, you may decide that this was not such a good idea at all. You may radically alter the idea to make it do what you want. You may even go back and look again at the idea you rejected. If you are really keen, you may check the Internet to see if there is a website that gives you a few ideas. You may also ask colleagues in the staff room (potential users) what they think of your idea. And now you have a design. Ask yourself, if you were to make it, 'What materials will I need?' 'What tools will I need?' 'Do I need to learn how to use one of those tools?' 'What would I do first?' 'If a saw will not cut it, is there an alternative?'.

Having gone through the process, think of the hard parts. Many people do not spend enough time clarifying the problem and deciding what exactly the solution should do. In this case, there are some sub-problems: the trap must attract a mouse into it, confine it without injury, be strong enough to keep it in, and let us release the mouse without being bitten. The next step is to look at these sub-problems. We know we have to attract the mouse into the trap. Our existing knowledge tells us to tempt it in with food. But which food is best? Do mice really prefer cheese? What do mice like best? Research with a book about mice would probably help here. The next sub-problem is, once the mouse is in the trap, how do we confine it there? We probably need what children call 'a special bit'. This special bit will let the mouse in but not let it out again. And then we have to think about letting the mouse out without it biting us. We also need to decide what materials we should use to make the trap: card would be no good; if the mouse peed with fright it would probably walk out through the damp card. Finally, you may have found that you followed one idea into a blind alley but you just could not switch your mind away from it enough to think of something else. Designers refer to this as psychological inertia. What can we do about these hard parts?

Designing skills

What skills does this involve? First, it means that the children have to understand the problem, need or task so that they know when they have solved the problem. This might sound obvious but it often takes some time to grasp what is needed. If they begin the journey too soon, they risk getting nowhere useful and, as a consequence, becoming very frustrated and demotivated. Second, they have to generate some ideas that sound as though they will solve the problem. This is the really creative part of the task and can be lots of fun. Third, the most promising of these ideas has to be developed further. Here, 'most promising' refers to an idea that seems likely, in the circumstances, to solve the problem and to do so safely. The various aspects of this idea are specified in sufficient detail for it to be turned into reality. Fourth, some forethought, or planning, is needed concerning the events that will turn this idea into a product, taking into account what is available.

When someone designs and makes something for themselves, these skills may be enough. In the real world, however, you often have to grasp other people's ideas and describe and explain yours to others. In other words, communication skills are also important. This means that children should acquire some essential vocabulary and use it. They need to exercise skills that help them understand explanations, such as asking questions, and that help them suggest alternatives. Various ways of expressing their thoughts need to be developed and used, such as talking, writing, drawing, and modelling.

Modelling is not about making model aeroplanes or ships to look at or play with. Modelling is about setting things up to try out an idea. Professional designers model in different ways. For instance, a car body designer may cut out the shape of a car in polystyrene while the team designing the mechanics of the seats may use a kit of plastic components to test the action of, say, a lever that lifts a seat. Similarly, a packaging technologist who has to make a plastic container for a light bulb shaped like Mickey Mouse may try the design in paper or card to make sure the light bulb fits snugly inside. Often, technologists also use computers to turn two-dimensional plans into three-dimensional shapes that they can rotate and view from different angles. When necessary the action of parts that are supposed to move can be tested with these digital models.

In the classroom, younger children should be encouraged to draw what they will make and use the drawing to identify the parts they must make and how they relate to one another. They should also try out parts of their design before they commit themselves to fixing them permanently in place. For example, children making a bed for one of the Three Bears should count the pieces in their pictures and note which pieces need to be long and which need to be short. When making the parts, they should try them next to one another to check their relative sizes and that those that should match do so.

The role of knowledge and understanding: two brief case studies

In the late nineteenth century, people used oil lamps or candles in the home. Thomas Edison in the USA saw the need for a better and safer source of light. He knew that electricity could make a piece of wire white hot and give off light but it soon melted. He had his workers try out one material after another, day after day, week after week. Eventually, they found one that glowed brightly for some time. That became the filament in Edison's first, commercial, light bulb.

In the nineteenth century, matches could be dangerous things, bursting into flames spontaneously. In England, John Walker saw the need for a safer match. Trying out one thing after another would have been an impossible task, particularly as the substances could be mixed in any proportions. But, with a knowledge of chemistry, he had some idea of what might work so he could narrow down the range considerably. In a relatively short time, Walker was able to make and sell a safety match from his chemist's shop.

The point is that knowledge can save time and effort. Edison knew how to make an electrical circuit and that a thin wire may glow when an electrical current flows through it. This gave him the idea for a solution but there was still a lot of work to do in finding a material that would last. His research was of the 'try it and see' kind. This takes time but, when the number of alternatives is relatively small, it is an option. Walker's knowledge of chemicals cut down the alternatives to a manageable number. In other words, knowledge and understanding can oil the process of designing. When this oil is missing, we could look for it or we could adopt the trial and error approach. Both can work although trial and error can be tedious, time-consuming and frustrating. A number of successful inventions have their origins in trial and error but, as teachers, we will want to take opportunities to develop knowledge and understanding, when appropriate.

In the mousetrap problem, knowing the size, weight, behaviour and preferences of mice could help a lot. We might have learned this in science or found it in a book. Similarly, having some knowledge of devices that could be triggered by a mouse and would keep it in the trap could point us in a fruitful direction. We might know this from earlier D&T work or have seen it in a toy. Knowledge like this is drawn on to help us solve the problem. (A simple solution to the mousetrap problem is outlined in the postscript at the end of the chapter.)

Making

Making is the process of turning a design into a product. Making is an essential part of the journey to the solution to a practical problem. Designing without making may be an amusing pastime, as when it leads to Heath-Robinson pictures or Chindogu ideas, but at the end of the day there is a mouse in the kitchen and we want a mousetrap, not an idea for one or even a picture of one. As with designing, the quality of a product benefits from thoughtful making. This is when actions are chosen because there is good reason to believe that they are likely to lead to a successful outcome. When you make, you are not some machine following a mechanical, fixed routine. You continually monitor the effects of what you do. If these effects are not what you had in mind, you pause and consider alternatives, change direction, do things in a different way, or adapt the design. In other words, your thoughtful making has a flexibility in it that leads to a good product.

The mousetrap problem revisited

Recall the humane mousetrap problem. Suppose you believe your design will work well if it was made of wood because this would make the mousetrap rigid and secure. You might ask, 'What tools should I use?'. (You recall that on the last occasion that you tried to make a hole in wood, it split.) 'Can I make it without splitting the wood?' 'How do I do that?' 'How can I do it safely?'. 'What do I do with the waste materials?' With an inclination to be thoughtful, you examine a strip of wood. It needs to be cut to size. You measure from one end and find you will have to make the cut where there is a knot. After a moment's thought, you measure from the other end and are able to avoid the knot. Now comes the sawing of the wood. You find the saw and bench hook. It can be difficult to start a neat cut in wood. You recall the trick: draw the saw blade over the wood a few times to start the cut. You are also aware that this needs care because the blade might skip or jump and cause an injury. And, there will be things that you did not anticipate. As you try the parts of your mousetrap, you find that the flap will have to be hinged very precisely if it is to swing down and hit the hole. A few attempts soon show you that this is not as easy as it seems. This could make the mouseflap action unreliable. Then it occurs to you that the mouseflap does not have to fit neatly into the hole. If it is bigger, it could simply fall and cover the hole, blocking the exit. You try it with a piece of thick card and see that it will be a more reliable solution. Now you make a larger flap and fit that. Making something to solve a problem is not a mindless task. As a teacher, your aim is to help children develop the habit of thoughtful making. Have them give reasons and justify what they do, monitor the effects of their actions and, where appropriate, look for other ways of doing things.

Note also that in making the mousetrap, the design was changed, a new idea was tested and incorporated into the product. Was this making or designing? The journey to a product cannot always be separated neatly into a beginning that is entirely designing and an ending that is entirely making. It is not wrong for a child to adapt a design, deviate from a plan, do things in a different way if there is good reason. What is not welcome is thoughtless, disorganized designing and making.

Making skills

At times, making skills and techniques may seem almost trivial to you but a child may not see it that way. Take using scissors. Using scissors is almost second nature to us but a child needs time and experience to build up this expertise. At the same time, a child has to build up a repertoire of techniques. For instance, if we want two identical card shapes, we know the trick of cutting out both shapes together but a very young child may not know how to do this. What skills are involved in making?

Children need to be able to select tools, materials and techniques that agree with one another and meet the needs of the task. They should also be able to measure, mark out, cut and shape various materials. Parts, materials and components often need to be joined or combined and children should learn to do this. Of course, all this has to be done safely. While you will always have responsibility for the children's safety, you will want them to be aware of what is involved, to have responsible attitudes, and to develop an inclination to work safely. Another concern to develop is for quality. Children should want their products to do what is intended, to do it reliably and effectively, and to be pleasing or satisfying to have around. Although planning is a skill described in designing, it is also a part of thoughtful making. You should foster this kind of thoughtfulness. Just as evaluation is a part of thoughtful designing, so it is also involved in making, both on the way to the product and in judging its quality when the child gets there. Thoughtfulness, of course, includes using tools safely.

Safe making

Making involves tools and our first concern has to be for working safely. Make time for talking about working safely and involve the children in it. Perhaps the earliest known picture about safety is on the wall of a tomb in Thebes. It shows someone remonstrating with three workers. One is polishing the top of a shrine and steadily moving backwards. Sooner or later, his co-worker will be pushed from the end of the tomb. In the meantime, the co-worker is chipping off pieces of stone onto the head of another person who has just dropped a stone hammer on his foot. Older children can make D&T safety posters like this themselves.

Children can learn some of the things designers have to think about by examining and discussing commonplace products and you will deliberately introduce these to your lessons. But tools themselves are products that meet a need. Talk about common tools and their origins and take opportunities to explain and demonstrate how to use them safely and what might happen if they are not used safely.

Many tools have a very long history and make interesting case studies that children can readily understand. For instance, hammers were as common in the Stone Age as they are now. The first hammer would probably be no more than a large pebble that would fit comfortably in the hand (but think of the dangers in that). Stones with a sharp edge served as axes and knives. Eventually ways of fitting handles were devised so that these tools took on their modern form. Knives were commonly made from flint because flakes of flint have very sharp edges. The Ancient Egyptians had stone hammers but they also had saws and chisels made from copper. These are very like the saws and chisels we use today except that now they are made of steel, a harder metal than copper. The Egyptians also had drills but these did not look like the modern hand-drill. Instead, a bow was used to turn the drill bit very like the way people used a bow-drill to make fire. Most of the handtools in common use today were 'invented' long ago. The only significant addition is the screwdriver.

Using ICT

Children in the primary school are also expected to develop Information and Communication Technology (ICT) skills. ICT has a dual role in D&T: it can be a means to an end and a part of the end itself. First, as a means to an end ICT can:

- support communication (by, for instance, using word processing and drawing packages);

- process information (as when the results of a survey are recorded on a spreadsheet which provides a summary);

- provide access to information (through the Internet or on a CD-ROM).

In addition, it can be used:

- to support the design process (with software intended for that purpose or by using the 'draw' facility that accompanies some word processing packages, or when the software enables modelling and simulation);
- to produce products (such as a greetings card, adhesive name badge, or calendar);
- to produce parts of a product ('wallpaper' for a model);

But, ICT can also be a part of the product itself, and be used:

- to control its operation (as when traffic lights are operated by a box of electronics).

Children should be introduced to ICT at an early age. Over time, their ICT vocabulary should be extended and they should become aware of the applications of ICT in everyday life (for example, the way barcodes are used in supermarkets and how sequences of action can be programmed into video recorders, washing machines and time switches). Nevertheless, you should remind yourself that ICT has its limitations. For instance, it is no substitute for the use of tools and direct contact with materials and components. Nor does it do much for developing interpersonal skills and relationships. Bear in mind that there are safety matters to consider as the hardware will probably be connected to the mains supply. Find out what the rules and regulations are and adhere to them. Also manage access to the Internet and e-mail to ensure no inappropriate materials are downloaded or people contacted. ICT can also help children with particular needs to learn in ways not listed above. This is outlined in Chapter 8.

Summary

Designing and making are about constructing solutions to practical problems or related tasks. It can be a rather erratic and messy process which involves a number of false starts. Nevertheless, we want children to go about it in a thoughtful way. Take care that your concerns are not only for pleasing drawings and written accounts. Marking can be more for presentation than for the quality of the ideas and how thoughtfully they have been developed. The important part of designing usually precedes the written work they hand in to you and may even follow it. If necessary, prompt or guide children's thinking to help them think productively. The longer-term aim is for children to develop the habit of doing this themselves so progressively wean them from your detailed support. Some designing skills to develop are:

- understanding and clarifying the problem, the need, or task;

- generating ideas, being creative towards a practical end;

- selecting an idea with good reason, developing ideas, considering safety;

- planning how to turn an idea into a product;

- evaluating and judging designs;

- communicating ideas, for example, by describing and explaining (orally and in writing), drawing and modelling.

Processes commonly associated with making products include:

- working with tools, materials and components;

- working safely;

- giving attention to quality, planning and evaluation.

We want to discourage a chaotic approach to designing and making and encourage thoughtful action so that tasks move forward towards a satisfactory conclusion.

Although designing and making have been presented separately, in practice, they are not always entirely separate on the way to a product. If you have a session for designing (and marking of work) followed by a session for making (and marking of the product) do not be so rigid about it that the children cannot develop ideas further. Nevertheless, this does not mean that you should accept thoughtless or haphazard designing and making. Note also that children can be impatient to use the tools and may give insufficient thought to what they will do with those tools. The *Appendix* has some worksheets that you may use to support thinking when designing.

Postscript

Garrison Keillor, in his book, *Leaving Home* (1988, p. 193), describes a humane mousetrap he used as a child on a farm in Minnesota. It comprised a bucket containing a little corn soaked in syrup. He placed the bucket under the stairs where mice jumped in, over-indulged on sweet corn then could not jump out.

CHAPTER 3

Teaching Designing and Making

Practical problems to practise on

Many of the tendencies, ways of working and skills we want to foster are best achieved through direct experience. Carefully chosen *designing and making activities* give children the chance to try it for themselves and learn in the process. Some designing and making activities do not need much preparation, either of minds or materials. For example, you might show that, in a packet of biscuits, the end ones are often broken. The packaging is inadequate. You challenge them to make a better packet for the biscuits. Many children have sufficient *knowledge* to draw on to solve this problem. They might even improve on it with a little research into using packaging and using paper to absorb shocks. Younger children may need a little teaching to prepare the way. You might, for instance, show them a range of papers and have them explore their properties. Then they might change their properties by bending, folding, and crumpling them. After this, you might show them examples of packaging and discuss their function. Now they are ready for the problem.

At times, the same approach will be necessary with older children. For example, you may have had them examine toys that use levers. You may follow that with some work using kits and have the children try levers in working models. Then you set the children the task of making a greetings card that uses levers to make parts move. The children can choose to make different kinds of greetings cards (such as, birthday, invitation to a school open day, congratulations) in different formats (such as, rectangular folded, unfolded, concertina, shaped) and depict different things on them. What aspect they choose to articulate is similarly open. They must explore the problem, design potential solutions, choose one for development and justify that choice, communicate the design in pictures and words, model moving parts, produce a plan of action, make the card and evaluate it and the process.

Practical skills to smooth the way

At times, you will need to focus on a particular skill and have the children practise it through a *focused activity* (also called a focused practical task although it can be about any aspect of designing and making, not just the use of tools). For instance, the children may be weak at collecting relevant information, planning a making sequence or sawing wood in broad strip form. You may decide that such skills need specific attention and practice. This is what a focused activity does.

Some knowledge and skills may be developed and practised quickly on a one-to-one basis and as the need for them arises. As you observe a child, you see he is struggling with a part of the task and that this is likely to impede progress. For instance, you see that he does not hold a nail in a way that allows it to be hit effectively and safely by a hammer. You show him how to grasp the hammer properly and hold the nail with pliers. After a quick demonstration, he tries it and succeeds. You monitor his skill for a while and satisfy yourself that he has acquired it.

Sometimes, however, just practising can be boring. Try to make it interesting by setting it in a *context*. Suppose you want younger children to practise sawing until they can do it with ease. You might tell them that Santa finds he is short of toys. All he has left for the elves to work with are some long strips of wood (30cm by 2cm by 1cm). What can he make? You show the group of children a flexible toy snake and suggest that this would make good use of the wood. How could they make the rigid piece of wood into a snake? You explore the task with the children and arrive at the conclusion that the strip needs to be sawn into fifteen pieces of equal size. You show the group how to use a saw and a bench hook and (when the strip is short) how to saw with the help of a small vice. You monitor the children's sawing and, as usual, pay particular attention to safety. The children produce the fifteen blocks, smooth them and glue them along a strip of felt or ribbon. With a felt tongue attached to the 'head' and some beads attached to the 'tail', the strip of wood becomes a bendy rattlesnake and the children have practised marking out equal-sized pieces and sawing and smoothing wood. This group of children are now ready for a problem that might be solved using this skill.

You can have children develop designing skills in the same way. For example, you could complain that your classroom does not work well; it always seems too crowded and untidy and everyone has to squeeze past the displays and that ruins them. You add that if you were a classroom designer, you would do things differently. Then the thought 'occurs' to you, 'Why don't we design the perfect classroom?'. Together, you and the class explore the problem. You collect ideas and then ask, 'Where might we find some more ideas?'. You have collected lots of kitchen brochures for the lesson. These show how wall and floor space can be used well and clever ways of storing things. 'Could we add any of these ideas to our own? How should we change them to make them right for a classroom?' Working with the children, you arrive at a possible Ideal Classroom. In the future, when the children seem short of ideas, you remind them how they obtained more in this task.

Bringing it all together

Figure 3.1 shows how these teaching devices can come together. Each benefits from a context that makes the work meaningful, purposeful and motivating. Contexts may, for example, come from a story, an event (contrived or otherwise), or something the children have been doing in another subject. If you can think of one context to cover all the tasks, so much the better but this is not always easy. Figure 3.1 also shows a *closing event*. A closing event that brings the work together and reviews it, consolidates it or extends it is likely to support learning.

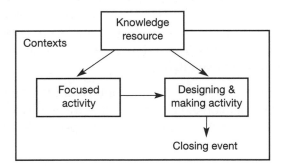

Figure 3.1 *A general structure for a block of work to develop designing and making capability.*

This sets out a general format for a block of work that could extend over several hours or lessons. As succeeding chapters will illustrate, it has many variations. For instance, there could be more than one focused activity or designing and making activity. Suppose you decide to try one of the blocks of work set out in those chapters. You get the children started but how do you help them make the most of the opportunity?

Helping children to design

Helping children to understand the problem or task

School inspectors have often found that designing skills are less well-developed than making skills. As the mousetrap shows, some aspects of designing can be demanding. In particular, children often have difficulty in grasping the problem or task and this can be the greatest, single difficulty. Telling them, even more than once, is often insufficient. If the problem is made meaningful, motivating and pitched at the right level, however, even young children can suggest relevant, sensible ideas for solving it.

With very young children, D&T-related opportunities for practical challenges are likely to arise as you lead an activity. If, for instance, your story is about the Three Blind Mice, you might ask, 'If the farmer's wife chases them out of the house, where are they to live?'. The story gives meaning to the problem and the children could model their ideas for solving it using wooden blocks to build a safe house (one that will not fall down) for the mice.

For older children, another way is to write the task, problem or challenge in the middle of the the board and open it up through questions. Using the mousetrap problem to illustrate the strategy (allowing that this particular problem may not be appropriate for the children you teach), you might begin with:

- *What's a mousetrap?* Real objects help people grasp problems. Here, you might show an example of a mousetrap or, at least, a picture of one.

- *Why do we want this mousetrap?* Mice spoil food. They can carry diseases. They breed quickly. But many people do not like to kill the mice and would prefer to catch them and release them outside. (This establishes the need. If this was with young children, you might refer to a story about mice or have older children research mice using books and ICT.)

- *What is a humane mousetrap?* We do not want to hurt the mouse and a humane trap lets us release it uninjured. (This means that the mousetrap must tempt the mouse to enter then 'somehow' keep it in – the 'special bit'. However it is kept in, it must be easy for us to let the mouse out.)

- *Who will use the mousetrap?* Anyone with a mouse problem can use it, old or young. (It would be better if the mousetrap was easy to set, even self-setting, if that is possible.)

- *Where is the mousetrap to be used?* Wherever mice are found in the house. On the floor. In a corner. Along the skirting board. Under cupboards. (This means that the mousetrap needs to be fairly compact.)

- *When is the mousetrap to be used?* The best time to set a mousetrap is at night because that is when mice tend to be active. (This means that if one is caught, it may be in this trap for several hours before it is released.)

- *What do mice like to eat?* This is knowledge to be acquired through research. Notice that these questions are, 'What?', 'Why?', 'When?', 'Who?', 'Where?'. Use these to construct a clear, mental picture of the characteristics of a solution: '*So, your mousetrap will* have *to ... and ... and ...*'

Helping children generate ideas

The next step is to deal with the 'How?' question. This is the creative bit that cannot be reduced to a step-by-step formula. The children have grasped the problem but there is a gap between it and the solution. How are they to bridge the gap? Even professional designers with years of experience can have difficulty with this. To make it easier, Genrich Altshuller, a Russian inventor, sorted thousands of solutions to practical problems into groups. In essence, his idea was that designers would find the group that was most like their problem. With a bit of luck, the solutions in that group would give the designer some good ideas to solve the problem. Altshuller's approach is too complex for children to use but it points the way to what you can do to help children when the going gets tough.

For instance, if the children were attempting the mousetrap problem, you could take Altshuller's place and help them think of ideas that might be useful or, if necessary, introduce some ideas. So, for instance, you might show them a picture of a cat-flap and discuss how it could be modified to become a drop-down door. You would ask how the door would be kept open and what the mouse would have to do to make it close behind it. The children may suggest propping the door open with a stick. The mouse is meant to dislodge it as it goes in. Instead of being faced with a blank sheet of paper and an infinite range of unknown possibilities, you have set the ball rolling with some rather rough and ready ideas that narrow the range a little. At times, as when making a bookmark, the children's prior knowledge and know-how is often enough. We pose the problem and let the children go straight to the designing. At other times, you need to point the way or help the children find information which points the way.

Choosing and developing an idea

A child may have several ideas to choose from. When this is the case, the child has to decide which is the most promising. To decide, you may need to help the child think about some of the following questions:

- what materials does it need?

- what materials are available?

- what tools does it need?

- what tools are available?

- what about safety?

- which looks as though it is most likely to work the way it should?

Note that while a child may be able to tell you what materials and tools will be needed for a given design, you may need to control what is available for the sake of safety. You may also have to show a child how to use a tool and give him or her the opportunity to practise with it. While you will want the child to think about safety (both in the designing and in the making), you must review this to satisfy yourself that everything the child will do or make is safe. These constraints may make the child's choice easier but there is still the last question. Which idea to develop further should not be a matter of whim or fancy so press the child to tell you why the chosen design is considered better than the alternatives.

Having chosen a design, it may need further development. Ask the child to explain how it will work and, in the process, identify parts that need more attention. For instance, if a child incorporates a mouseflap in the design, what will stop the mouse simply pushing the flap up to get out again? If it would help, encourage the child to model parts of the design. Thought should also be given to appearance and how the product will be finished.

This is a good place for a few words about drawing. We tend to think of the accurately drafted drawings that engineers prepare for a manufacturer. This is when a drawing is being used as a device to support communication. But drawings can also help children think. Children tend to use drawings spontaneously in this way so encourage them to apply it to help their designing. Have the children sketch their ideas and work out what the parts will do on paper. Such drawings should not be judged as pieces of art work. They are to make what the child is thinking more concrete and serve as extra working memory. As such, they are likely to include lots of changes of mind but they help the child to clarify thoughts. They may also let you see what is going on and you can use them to help the child make progress. When the child has arrived at a promising design, you may have them turn the drawing into a neater version, perhaps using ICT, then use the drawing to explain the design to others. But remember that the earlier drawings may tell you more about the child's thinking.

Like drawing, modelling can also help children think and help them to communicate with others. It turns thoughts into a concrete, three-dimensional object that can be manipulated to see what it does. Unlike drawing, however, modelling is not something that most primary school children do spontaneously. You will generally need to introduce it and practise it with them. So, for instance, with the cat-flap above, you might model how it works using card. Models do not have to include everything in the design. They are usually most useful for exploring how particular parts will work or relate to other parts.

Helping children to plan ahead

Thinking ahead is a part of thoughtful designing. Planning is the formal version of that. Young children should be able to tell you what they will do next and what they will do after that. Older children can be expected to produce a sequence of actions which will lead to the product and, perhaps, mention one or two alternatives if things do not go according to plan at certain points. Obviously, you move progressively from the former to the latter. Plans can have various forms and it may maintain interest if you vary what you have the children do. Plans can be, for example:

- an oral listing (for younger children and those with writing difficulty);
- a sequence of pictures;

- a written account;

- a diary;

- a list;

- a list of instructions, written as for someone else to use;

- a checklist, to be ticked when each action is completed;

- a flow-chart;

- a flow-chart with branches for alternatives.

Where children can use one, a word processor is often helpful in preparing plans as it allows re-ordering in a quick and easy way. (Some examples of planning support sheets are in the *Appendix*.)

Helping children evaluate their designing

Evaluation in designing is generally not something that is done at the end but is a part of the on-going process. So, for example, the flap of a child's mousetrap model does not fall every time. Sometimes, it stays upright even when the supporting peg has been knocked away. Is this going to be a problem in the final version made from wood? If so, what can I do about it? Later, the child thinks of a more complex release mechanism that might be more reliable. Will it be too difficult to make? The child also considers the external appearance of the mousetrap and judges it to be rather ugly. Similarly, the interior is lacking in comfort for the mouse. An attempt is made to make the mousetrap more attractive and comfortable.

This kind of on-going evaluation is at the heart of thoughtful designing. Of course, you may have to bring the need for evaluation to a child's attention as designing proceeds. But, it is not simply a case of judging whether something is good or bad, reliable or unreliable, attractive or unattractive. The aim is to stimulate thought that makes the bad better, the unreliable more reliable and the unattractive more attractive.

What can distinguish more able from less able children is an inclination to work thoughtfully in this way. So, for example, some children may have a chaotic approach to problem-solving. They tend to be passive or inactive learners with little inclination to evaluate what they do spontaneously. Giving them a lot of practice in designing is not, in itself, enough. You need to structure the task into a sequence of small steps (for instance, written on cards), draw attention to that structure, expect the child to reproduce that structure in the future, and eventually have them adapt it to suit a new situation. With such children, success is important and believing that success came from their own efforts is essential.

Learning about designing from products

Designing, of course, is not just something the children do. Talking about products can be very instructive and interesting. This is something you can do even with very young children. For instance, you might show them a simple, mechanical toy and have them explain how it works. If you have an old toy from your childhood, this is 'history' for very young children. You might show it and have them compare it with a more recent version of the same toy. For older children, there are many everyday products that you might talk about. A number were mentioned in Chapter 1. Some key questions are:

- 'What does it do?'

- 'Why do people need it?'

- 'Why is is made from that material?'

- 'What makes it look/feel good?'

For example, you may be able to show an old toaster and a modern toaster. The questions now are:

- 'How are they different?'

- 'Which one is better?'

- 'What makes it better?'

Not everything needs to be familiar at the outset. So, as an example of homes from around the world or from earlier times, you might show older children a picture of a house built on stilts over water. You could ask, for instance:

- Why is it built over water like this? What problems could it solve?

- Would it be hard to build a house like this? What might be the hardest part? How do you think they did it?

- What might happen after the house had been standing in water for a long time? How would you build a house like this so that its stilts would not rot in the water?

- The walls are made of woven branches. How would you cook food over a fire in a house like this?

- Would you like to live in a house like this? Why?

- We started by talking about the problems a house like this might solve. Could you solve the problems in a different way?

Helping children to work with tools, materials and components

Class organization

Some teachers have the whole class do D&T at the same time. Others are in the habit of having small groups take turns to do D&T. A better way of working is to vary the approach to suit the task. If, for instance, you want the children to design and make name badges, they are likely to use scissors or snips and card or soft plastics. This is likely to be the sort of task that the whole class could do together. It also means that you can introduce the task, prepare the way, interact and pull things together at the end without having to divide your attention. Similarly, talking about products is often best done as a whole class activity. It is economical with your time as you do not have to repeat introductions and plenary sessions.

If, however, you plan a task that will involve a new skill, such as sawing or drilling, you are likely to find it easier to work with a succession of small groups. This a better way of working for one-to-one instruction on the use of a tool and supervision of its practice. Later, when the skill is well-established and the children can work safely, you may increase the group size. This, of course, assumes that you have enough tools to do that.

This flexible way of working means that the children will generally have to work at their tables for whole class activities. For group work, however, you may have the option of a dedicated work space for D&T. Dedicated work areas can have the advantage of being equipped and fitted out for the task. Everything has its place and everything is in its place. A disadvantage can be that plenary sessions that pull together and review learning can be more difficult to fit in unless you make a conscious effort to do so.

D&T is an activity where you need to have the children in clear view. When the whole class are taught together, many parts of the teaching are just like any other subject. The children work at the tables, individually, in pairs or in groups. You introduce the topic and discuss it with them. The children engage in designing and planning and you support them as they do so. Even using tools and materials can often be a whole class event with the children working at their tables. Encourage the children to work in an organized and tidy manner and set an example yourself. You could, for example:

- have the children trace the outline of the tools they are using on an A3 sheet of paper and place it in the centre of the table: the tools are put in their places on the paper and returned there after use;

- have the children organize their work using a tray: the tools (and materials, if you wish) are kept in that tray;

- have the children dispose of waste materials appropriately: put a shoe box or something similar on each table for that.

Tools

With very young children, you will probably put out only those tools they need for the task in hand, such as safe scissors. Demonstrate the correct way to hold and use a tool. Supervise the children closely as they acquire the skill and give one-to-one support. Always keep all the children in clear sight and intervene if anything unsafe develops. With other children, you could add tools to a toolbox as the children acquire the skills to use them. This means that the children will increasingly have to choose an appropriate tool from the range available. Check that all tools are present after use. Look for any that need repair or replacement and remove them from use. A tool kit to meet the needs of D&T-related activities for very young children or D&T in the primary school does not have to be large. Here are some items you are likely to find useful. Those you might consider for very young children have an asterisk.

For cutting and shaping materials:

- *safe scissors (for paper, thin card and fabrics; consider safe, self-opening scissors for very young children);

- *safety snips (child sized, for cutting card and thin sheets of plastic, see, for instance, the TTS website: www.tts-shopping.com);

- *hole punch (for punching holes for axles, string or wool);

- junior hacksaw (for cutting lengths of strip wood);

- wood rasp (a very coarse file that can shape wood held in a vice);

- pliers (for holding and for cutting).

For fixing materials together:

- *stapler (for fixing a thin material to another);

- hammer (approximately 300g or 1/2 lb) with nails and tacks;

- glue gun (cool glue variety);

- *pot of PVA adhesive and glue spreader.

For holding items so that they can be worked:

- small vice (for holding things firmly);

- bench hook (for holding strip wood on a table for cutting with a saw).

For measuring and marking materials:

- *safety rule (this has a trough down its length for fingers).

For storing tools:

- *plastic tool box (to hold all these tools and that can take a small padlock to keep them secure).

You will also need tools for clay, foodstuffs and fabrics. Tools and similar implements used for foodstuffs should be kept in hygienic conditions apart from the other tools.

For working with clay:

- *spatulas of various kinds (for shaping the clay);

- *plastic plates (to carry the clay while it is being worked);

- *roller made of thick plastic or wood (for rolling out the clay).

For working with foodstuffs:

- *safe items associated with food processing (for example, bowls, plates, spoons, biscuit shape-cutters).

For working with fabrics:

- *pot of fabric adhesive;

- tape measure;

- a variety of needles and sewing threads;

- needle threader;

- thimble.

You may also find certain additional items useful although multiples of them may not be needed:

- drill-stand (to help children hold and manipulate the hand-drill);

- *self-opening safe scissors (having a loop between the handles so that they open by themselves: they can be easier to manipulate than conventional scissors);

- clamps (to hold items to a table top or together).

Many tools, like hammers and saws, suit right and left-handed people equally. You could try to find scissors and hand-drills that are better suited to left-handed children. Which tools should you make available? Often, teachers of young children avoid using tools like the junior hacksaws on grounds of safety. Your school will probably have a policy or rule about progression in tool use and you should obey it. Some schools begin to teach the use of tools like the junior hacksaw with 5 – 7 year olds but only through one-to-one instruction and with direct supervision. Again, always obey the school rules on tool use. When in doubt, seek advice from the subject co-ordinator or the headteacher and, especially if you are new to teaching, err on the side of caution.

Materials and components

One aim of elementary D&T education is to have the children learn about a variety of materials and components. The materials and components most frequently used are:

- paper and card (for example, tissue, crêpe, sugar, cartridge, greaseproof, metallized, corrugated);

- woods (for example, jelutong from Malaysian managed woodlands or the cheaper pine equivalent, twigs, lollipop sticks) avoid hardwoods like oak and mahogany;

- plastics (there are many kinds of plastic but the easier ones to shape are generally those from food containers, such as ice-cream cartons; avoid the hard, brittle and sharp-edged plastics);

- metal foils (for example, wrappers from sweets, cooking foils; avoid thick foils that produce sharp edges);

- fabrics (for example, pressed materials like felt, knitted materials made from wool, and woven materials made from cotton and other fibres);

- clay (potter's clay and, if possible, have the children compare it with clay they have dug up themselves; other clay-like materials are available that do not need to be fired);

- foods and their components (for example, fruit, flour, concentrated drinks, milk, cheese, yoghurt, herbs and spices);

- electrical components (for example, torch light bulbs, wires, batteries, electronic control devices. The last are unlikely to be useful with very young children);

- recycled items (for example, kitchen roll tubes, shoe boxes, cereal packets, coffee jar lids).

To begin with, you will tend to make a limited range of materials available and widen it over time. So, for instance, you might begin with paper of the size and thickness that suit the task in hand. Later, you could offer a range of papers: tissue, crêpe, greaseproof, drawing, sugar, and newsprint. Some of these should suit the task better than others. Of course, children are not always economical with materials. They will, for instance, cut a circle of card from the middle of a large sheet. Have them consider why this is not a good thing to do and what they should do instead. Foodstuffs need special consideration. Buy what is needed on the day it will be used and keep it in a refrigerator until it is needed. There are often school and Local Education Authority rules and advice from educational organizations about foodstuffs and recycled materials. For instance, toilet roll tubes may seem a good substitute for kitchen roll tubes but they are generally not used as they may be contaminated. In other words, make yourself familiar with what is and is not allowed.

Classrooms for very young children often have blocks which can be used for building structures like houses and castles. There may also be a large-scale construction kit. Some include a small-scale version for modelling what the children will make. For older children, there are kits which are intended to develop knowledge of, for example, levers, cams and gears. Usually, they do this by having the child make a working model which incorporates these mechanisms.

These kits can have a dual function. First, they provide making activities that teach the children about aspects of D&T. Second, they can be used to model what the children plan to make to check that it will work as expected. So, for instance, a child may develop an idea for a 'picker upper' for someone with a bad back using a Lego® or Meccano® kit then make the real thing using strips of wood. In the same way, an electricity kit from the science cupboard may be used to try out the design of a circuit for a flashing light in a lighthouse. Equally, components from the electricity cupboard (such as, light bulbs in holders, batteries, switches and wires with crocodile clips on the ends) can be used in designs that involve other things.

A word about children using kits may be helpful. Some children may have had experience of construction kits at home. They know how to use them and what they can do, and can use them fairly quickly to test their ideas. Others, however, will not have had that experience. Give them time to examine the kit and to try making things before expecting them to solve problems with it. The second point is a practical one: place the kit in a tray and have the children construct with it in the tray. This reduces the likelihood that parts will be lost.

Helping children to work safely

Your prime concern is that the children will work safely and will not injure themselves or others. But working safely also means teaching children to think about and avoid unsafe ways of working themselves – in other words, having them acquire a lifeskill and a valuable habit – another aspect of thoughtful making. Children, classrooms, materials and tools vary so it is not possible to provide a specific list of dos and don'ts. Your school and Local Education Authority will have rules and regulations you must follow. Your subject co-ordinator will also be able to provide advice on specific points. In addition, there are very useful booklets on safety in D&T. Here are some general points you should consider:

- buy, read and act upon the advice in a book on safety in D&T (see Further Reading);

- check all tools frequently for damage and rectify or replace damaged items (it can be useful to attach cards to tool boxes to record the date when you checked them – this helps to avoid missing a box and reminds you to check them);

- always show children the correct way to use a tool before they use it then ensure that they use it correctly subsequently (for example, children often want to grip a hammer near its head but, if they miss their target, they risk hitting their knuckles);

- always check the materials and components you provide, removing those that are hazardous or faulty (for example, pieces with sharp points, splinters of wood and broken torch light bulbs);

- remember that different ways of working may be necessary with different materials to ensure safety (for example, food technology involves a high level of hygiene and even though common household items are used, children may not use them safely; do not give children access to ovens and other heating devices);

- ensure that the adults you have in the classroom know how you want the children to use the tools, how they should support your work and attend to matters of safety);

- when thinking about safety, do not forget your own safety and the safety of other adults (such as that of cleaners and caretakers who must remove waste materials);

- make yourself, other adults and the children familiar with what to do in the event of an accident, however minor (your school is likely to require that some formal record is kept);

- keep up-to-date on matters of classroom safety by reading bulletins produced by your Local Education Authority, professional and similar organizations (no list like this can ever hope to be complete because your class will vary from year to year and what you do will change).

Involve the children in your concerns for a safe environment. Have them think about potential hazards and how to avoid them. For instance, you could:

- use discussion to agree a short list of rules that will be made into a safety poster for the classroom (the class might consider the value of keeping the work area clear, tidy and uncluttered, the need to dispose of waste properly and without filling the air with dust, how to recognize and bring damaged tools to your attention, and never using tools to point at someone);

- give the children pictures of people using tools and have them identify the hazards in tool use and ways of working;

- have the children do classroom safety audits to see if they can identify hazards more broadly (and then think of ways of eliminating them or, at least, warning people of them).

You may be offered a variety of unwanted tools by helpful parents. Be very selective about what you put into the children's tool boxes. Reject tools that are not in a good condition or are not safe for the children to use and avoid tools that are too large or heavy for the children. As a rule, stick to the conventional tools used in the primary classroom. Helpful parents may also offer materials but, again, be selective. Even soft wood needs to be in convenient sizes and if you are not able to cut it to more manageable sizes, assume that the children are likely to have difficulty with it too. Also avoid manufactured materials like MDF (medium density fibre board). It is generally difficult for children to work with and the dust can be hazardous. Also find out if any children are allergic to certain materials and foodstuffs and avoid them.

Parents can be particularly helpful when you provide them with a list of useful items you will need (for example, kitchen roll tubes and balls of wool).

Helping children to work for quality

There are a variety of ways products can be finished in the classroom. For instance, a child might:

- colour a product using water-based paints, crayons, inks, or coloured pencils;
- paste on a patterned paper (ready-made or generated using ICT);
- apply a textured finish using sand and adhesive;
- apply a sparkling finish using glitter and adhesive;
- clad a surface with a fabric;
- rub a surface until smooth;
- smooth a surface then rub in shoe polish and buff it with a duster.

Children need to learn that some finishes work better on some materials than on others. For instance, a water-based paint may look good on new wood but it can make card products warp, distort and become useless. There are also skills associated with applying particular finishes. These need to be taught and practised. If these skills are neglected, products can look worse and function less well after they have been 'finished' than they did before. Again, looking at and talking about the finishes applied to real-world artefacts, such as toys, can be instructive for children.

Quality, of course, includes the extent to which the product does what it was intended to do. Some products also need to be reliable and durable. So, for example, if the mousetrap is meant to be disposable, the child should at least try to make sure it will work when a mouse goes into it. You may need to remind children of the primary goal of the task.

Helping children to plan

Although children may tell you what they will do next or have a step-by-step plan on paper, even the best plans leave things unsaid. Take for example, 'Step 5: Fix the parts of the buggy together'. Which parts should be fixed first? Similarly, 'Step 6: Fit wheels to buggy'. Unless children are thoughtful about it and think through the fine detail as they go along, they will end up gluing both wheels on the axle before they try to thread the axle onto the axle supports. Then there is, 'Step 7: Paint buggy and paste on Go – Faster stripes made on the computer'. The child needs to allow for the unstated drying time between painting and pasting. One 'fine detail plan' would be to paint the buggy then make the Go – Faster stripes while the buggy is drying. These developments may be carried in the mind. By thinking ahead, children can avoid difficulties and save time. They may learn by experience or you may need to draw it gently to their attention.

Helping children to evaluate

As in designing, children need to evaluate their work as it progresses. This is an aspect of thoughtful making. As they make various parts, they should be inclined to try them loosely to see if they fit or relate as intended. If, for instance, they find that the nails they were using to hinge the flap will not go into the wood straight, should they persist and probably produce a poor product or think of another way of hinging the flap?

But now, with the mousetrap finally made and looking good on the table comes the ultimate evaluation. Does it work as intended? The children should now test the trap (humanely, on a small ball) and gauge its effectiveness. Does the mousetrap flap work as it should: sometimes, about half the time, almost every time? Does the ball roll out to freedom when the trap is tilted? How many times could the trap be used? Is it disposable? What about its appearance? Would its human owner be happy to leave it out on the floor? These questions clearly reflect upon the quality of the finished product.

Helping children pull it all together: the closing event

Merely completing the tasks above is not, of course, the end of it. We want this fairly limited experience to make a difference but no one is a perfect learning machine. Learning can be more or less fragmented unless we help the children make sense of it, tie it together, relate it to what they already know and practise it in new contexts. This means that you will need to:

1. Check on and review the quality of the learning, making good any deficits.

2. Tie this new and still fragile learning to other things the children know.

3. Provide further work that exercises the learning in new contexts.

The first of these can be done in a plenary session with the children. This can be a natural part of the work where you have the children talk about their solutions to the problem, and demonstrate and evaluate them. Some questions could be:

● 'What was our problem?'

● 'Tell me why you chose to make a ...'

- 'Did it solve the problem?'

- 'Show me your picture of what you were going to make. Is what you made exactly like this?' 'Why not?'

- 'What was the hardest part to make?' 'Why was that?'

- 'If you were to make it again, what would you do differently?'

The second can be done by, for instance, asking the children if there is anything that the device reminds them of. 'How is it the same?' 'How is it different?' You may have to direct their attention to everyday examples of the mechanism or artefact. For instance, if the children have constructed something that involves a crank handle on a wheel, then the pedals on a bicycle and the winder on a mechanical whisk from the kitchen may be examples the child can think of. When appropriate, also have the child relate what they have done to earlier work in D&T and in other subjects. 'Why did you choose that for the roof of the bird feeder?' 'How do you know it will keep the water out?' 'What else did we test in science that was like that?'

For the third, have one or two items set aside to show the children. For instance, after activities that included making a bendy snake, you may have another bendy toy. Have the child explore and talk about it. Could she have used that idea? What would she have had to do differently? Can she think of a third way of making something bendy? What might that be good for? If you have another problem in an interesting context for the children, it is sometimes possible to move into another designing and making activity at this point. Of course, once the children have some facility with reading and writing, you may also give them some pencil and paper tasks but make these require thought. Here are some examples:

- The school has a litter problem and the children have been designing and making a litter bin and Keep Our School Tidy posters. Here are some closing event questions you might use:

  a) Bins can be made of different materials. Some have solid sides and are made of plastic. Some have solid sides and are made of metal. Some have mesh sides (like a net) and are made of metal.

     (i)   Which would be the best one to use for something hot?
     (ii) Which would be the best one to use for something wet?
     (iii) Which would be the best one to use for very small things?
     (iv) Which would be the best one to use for crumpled paper?

  b) Can you invent another kind of bin? Grandma has an old-fashioned coal fire and has to use sticks to light it. Invent a bin for her to store her sticks. It must keep them dry and let her get them out easily. Remember, she cannot bend over easily. Draw a picture of your bin and explain how it will work.

- After doing some designing and making of packages for solid objects, the teacher gives the children a worksheet showing pictures of different kinds of 'packages' for liquids. These are: a fizzy drinks can, a milk carton, a window cleaning spray, and a washing-up liquid bottle. The pictures do not indicate the contents. Here are the accompanying questions:

  a) What do you think is in each container?
  b) Why are the containers different?
  c) What makes each container good for its job?

- Following some simple work on hydraulics and pneumatics, using syringes and tubes, a child is given a pump action soap dispenser and has to write answers to the following:

  a) Is this better than a bar of soap?
  b) Why do you think that?
  c) How does it work?

Using ready-made products in this way can make children aware of some of the problems and solutions in designing and making. Learning from products is one of the subjects discussed in Chapter 7.

Summary

This chapter set out things to think about in planning in order to develop designing and making skills. You will need to consider:

- the knowledge resource (Is it present? Will I need to teach it? Will I need to help the children convert science knowledge into device knowledge? Can the children find it for themselves?);

- focused activities (Is one needed? Will one do? What will the context be?);

- designing and making activities (What will it be? How will I present it (context)?);

- the closing event (How will I draw things together? How will I consolidate the learning? How might I extend the learning?).

Learning is also likely to benefit from support during the process of designing and making, particularly with help in understanding the nature of the task.

CHAPTER 4

D&T-Related Activities for 3 – 5 Year Olds

This chapter describes D&T-related activities for the early years, foundation or 3 – 5 stage. The oldest of these children will probably be in the primary school reception class. D&T is rarely seen as a distinct subject in this stage so activities are described as D&T-related to reflect that. These very young children can be given many opportunities to engage in D&T-related activities. There will often be times when you have to help to maintain direction and to support learning. The timing of these interventions needs to be finely judged. Watch for mounting frustration, declining interest or the need to develop a skill or knowledge and then intervene to ensure that activities are successful and that the children benefit from them. There may be teaching assistants, parents or carers who will help you in the classroom. These helpers should be welcomed but plan what they will do and prepare them for the task. They will then be more satisfied with their role, they will want to help again and the children will gain more from their presence. They should not simply do the tasks for the children as that would greatly reduce their benefit.

Examples

In the following examples the *Starting Points* provide a context for simple practical tasks. The *Activity* describe a task and *Follow-up* suggests a further activity. *Prior experience* describes useful knowledge resources or skills. Although some *Learning opportunities* are listed, these cannot be exhaustive and you could use the activities in other ways. This is a simplified version of the structure described in the previous chapter to suit very young children and the nature of the D&T-related activities they might do.

At the end of the chapter, a stock of teaching ideas is provided. You can select activities from these to suit the children's needs and capabilities. These are not in the same detail as the exemplars but can be treated similarly. Stories and visits are particularly useful when working with very young children. They provide meaningful backgrounds, starting points and contexts. The children can learn from them, relate to them and gain purpose for the activities they do. A Planning Sheet to help you develop such ideas, including ideas you have yourself, is provided at the end of the *Appendix*.

Paper bag puppets

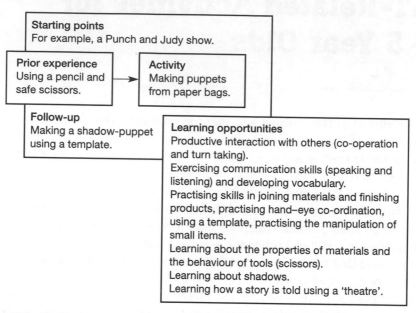

Figure 4.1 *Outline of an activity to do with paper bag puppets.*

Prior experience

You could use Paper Bag Puppets widely with young children as the knowledge and skill demands are low.

The Starting Point

Try a simple 'Punch and Judy' show using a cardboard box and some glove-puppets. Make the upper half of the box like a television screen by cutting a rectangular hole in the front. Cut a similar hole in the bottom half of the back of the box. Place the box on a table and insert your puppets from the back. Use them to tell a story. It does not have to be the Punch and Judy story. For instance, it could be the story of Humpty Dumpty or something that suits the puppets you have. This introduces the concept of the puppet. After the story, show the children how the puppets are made and operated.

Activity

You need a paper bag for each child. The bag should be small enough for the children to insert a finger and thumb in the two corners. Show the children how to manipulate the paper bag puppet but, after they try it, proceed quickly to the next step. Ask how they might make it look like a person or another animal. Show them how to cut out and glue on coloured pieces of paper to represent eyes, nose and mouth and ears. They could also use wool or a furry fabric for hair. Let the children try the puppets in your cardboard box theatre. Encourage them to have their puppets 'speak'. Have the children play together in small groups using their puppets.

Follow up

Demonstrate a cut-out shadow-puppet. Ask the children how it works. Encourage them to explain by using their hands to cast shadows. Ask what makes shadows and then what makes the best shadows. Use your shadow-puppets to tell a simple short story (see below). Later, have the children make cut out animal figures by drawing around simple card templates of animals. Let them hold their figures in the light so that they cast shadows. Encourage them to move the figures in ways that make them look 'alive'.

'Eat me!' said the fish: A shadow-puppet story

Cut out two shapes in card to use as shadow-puppets, one of a crocodile with an open mouth and one of a large fish. Attach them to lollipop sticks and hold them so that their shadows face one another. The story goes something like this:

'Hello!' said the crocodile.

'Hello!' said the fish.

'Had much to eat today?' asked the crocodile.

'Oh, yes,' said the fish.

'Me, too,' said the crocodile, moving closer, 'I couldn't eat another thing.'

'That's good,' said the fish, 'I thought you might want to eat me.'

'No, I don't want to eat me!' said the crocodile. 'That would be silly.'

'You silly crocodile,' said the fish. 'I said, "eat ME", not "eat YOU".'

'How kind!' said the crocodile, 'I thought you'd never ask!'

Snap went the crocodile and the fish was gone.

Learning opportunities

There are opportunities to develop social skills, as when the children co-operate in their play with their paper bag puppets. The play will only work for them if they allow some turn-taking so that each puppet has its say and action. Attention skills are practised in this play and in listening to the puppet stories. In addition, they must persist if they are to make a puppet themselves. The activity involves listening to stories and making their own puppets 'speak' so there are opportunities to develop language and communication skills. The children also develop some knowledge of how materials like paper behave and they can add to their shaping and joining skills with paper, manipulating objects and exercising hand–eye co-ordination. They can also add to their knowledge of how light behaves and how shadows are produced. The puppets give them an opportunity to be creative in how they use them in play.

Bugs in a flap

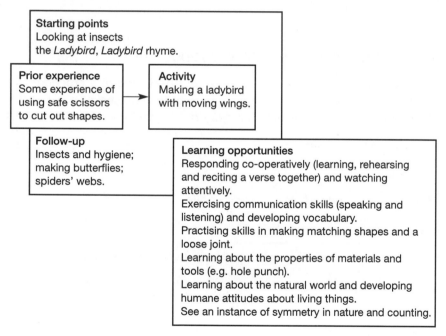

Figure 4.2 *Outline of an activity to make a bug with moving parts from card.*

Prior experience

The making task may be better suited to those children with more experience of cutting out shapes.

The Starting Point

The starting point with the best learning opportunities is direct experience. If you find a ladybird, take the opportunity to collect it in a transparent plastic jar and have the children observe it. If possible, collect a ladybird when the children are with you so that they see it in its natural habitat. Very young children are often unafraid of insects, especially ladybirds and butterflies. Take care to reinforce that feeling. Have the children make pictures of ladybirds and cut them out. Attach their pictures to a large picture of a plant. With the children, release the ladybird, explaining why that is the right thing to do, encouraging respect for living things.

Activity

With the help of a template, have the children make a ladybird's body. Provide one template for the 'wings' (strictly speaking, they are wing cases; the wings are under them). When the children have made one 'wing', support their thinking so that they make a matching second 'wing'. Show them how to use a hole punch and help them locate a suitable place to punch the holes in the wings and body. Open the paper fasteners slightly for the children so that they can use them more readily. Make sure they use them safely and with care or fit them yourself. Most will tighten the fastener too much and you should slacken it for them so that the wings will open. Black wool attached with adhesive tape or PVA adhesive will make feelers for the ladybird (figure 4.3). You could then ask the children how they might make legs and let them use the wool for that. Finally, have the children count the spots and make the same number and pattern on their models.

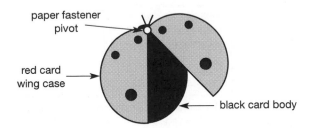

Figure 4.3 *The ladybird.*

Follow-up

Have the children learn and recite the Ladybird rhyme together:

Ladybird, Ladybird

Ladybird, ladybird,

Fly away home

Your house is on fire

And your children all gone.

Some insects, like houseflies, carry harmful germs. It would be useful to tell the children that insects are to look at, not handle. They should also be told to keep insects away from food. Spiders are not insects but they catch insects in their webs and eat them. One damp morning, show the children a spider's web. Water droplets make its structure clear. If necessary, spray the web gently with water. Have them draw a spider's web and make spiders from black pipe cleaners or wool to fix on their webs.

Learning opportunities

Have the children give their full attention to the ladybird and its actions. You can support this by talking about it as the children watch. For instance, have them name the colour and, with you, count the spots and the legs. Afterwards, have them 'be a ladybird' for a minute. There are also opportunities to practise responding in unison when they count and when they recite the verse with you. The making of the model ladybird practises cutting skills and also the making of a loose joint. Decorating it to make it look like the real thing involves matching and symmetry. This is an opportunity to learn about the natural world and, importantly, see and acquire caring attitudes towards it. There is no need to distinguish between insects and spiders at this stage.

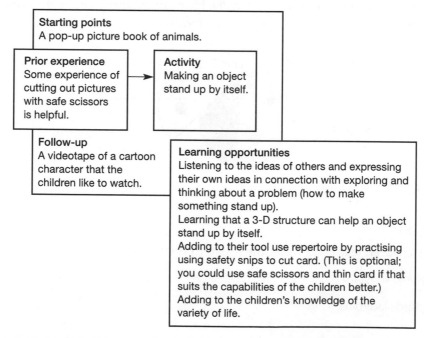

Figure 4.4 *Outline of an activity to make card animals stand up by themselves.*

Animals that stand up by themselves

Prior experience

Not much formal prior experience is needed but the children should have reached a stage where they would like a model that stands up by itself (see figure 4.4).

The Starting Point

Use a pop-up picture story book about animals to engage the children's attention and have them think about animals. Show some animal pictures. Which can they name? How big are they? What do they eat?

Activity

Provide some animal pictures. Have the children draw and cut out an animal. Ask them if they will stand up and how we might make them stand up. Show the children how to make a dog from card. Have the children tell you what features it should have and draw them on the card (for example, eyes, mouth, nose, ears). Attach a tail made from wool. Show the children that we have a problem: the dog will not stand up. Cut along the dotted lines in the diagram and slot in two pieces of card to serve as legs. Show that the dog stands up by itself. Have the children do the same for an animal of their choice. Put them all together to make a zoo or pet shop.

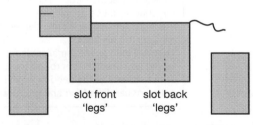

slot front   slot back
'legs'   'legs'

Figure 4.5 *Parts of a dog that stand up by itself.*

Follow–up

Have the children sit together to watch a favourite cartoon character on a videotape. Afterwards, provide a number of cartoon character pictures for the children to cut out. Have them glue the pictures to a rectangular piece of card. Prop them up to make a display but let them fall down. Ask what they could do to make them stand up. Take and accept ideas. Show the children some tubes and ask if tubes might help. If necessary, illustrate their use by cutting slits in them to hold the cartoon figures upright.

Learning opportunities

These activities provide opportunities for the children to listen together and engage in talk about what they have heard. The introduction can illustrate the variety of animals in the world. They also have a chance to practise listening to the ideas of others and to express their own ideas when they think about how to solve the problem of making an animal stand up. The solution extends their knowledge of what helps things stand up and practises their cutting and shaping skills.

Making better biscuits

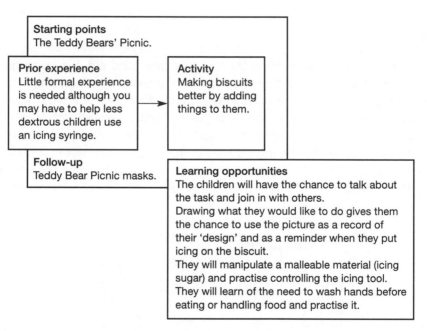

Starting points
The Teddy Bears' Picnic.

Prior experience
Little formal experience is needed although you may have to help less dextrous children use an icing syringe.

Activity
Making biscuits better by adding things to them.

Follow-up
Teddy Bear Picnic masks.

Learning opportunities
The children will have the chance to talk about the task and join in with others.
Drawing what they would like to do gives them the chance to use the picture as a record of their 'design' and as a reminder when they put icing on the biscuit.
They will manipulate a malleable material (icing sugar) and practise controlling the icing tool.
They will learn of the need to wash hands before eating or handling food and practise it.

Figure 4.6 *Outline of an activity using foodstuffs.*

Prior experience

Little formal prior experience is needed. Some control is needed when applying icing and this activity gives children the chance to develop it. Check for food allergies and respect food preferences and prohibitions (see also *Using food*, in the section describing *D&T-related activities in outline for the 3 – 5 stage).*

The Starting Point

The Teddy Bears' Picnic provides a context. Use Teddy bears, card plates and a table cloth as props. Set them out and ask what the children think it is for. Sing *The Teddy*

Bears' Picnic song with the children. Afterwards, direct attention to the empty plates and point out that the Teddy Bears need something to eat.

Activity

This activity also provides the opportunity to talk about simple matters of hygiene when working with food. Talk with the children about hand-washing before meals and when preparing food. To make the point, have the children wash their hands before proceeding.

You may prefer to use tubes of ready-to-use icing. The icing is available in various colours and comes with several nozzles. Show the children how to pipe icing onto plain biscuits to make faces. Sprinkle vermicelli and hundreds and thousands to make hair. You could use chocolate buttons for eyes. Show the children some blank biscuits (ones that do not break easily) and tell them that they will make faces on their biscuits too. But, first, before they do, they have to draw on paper the faces that they would like to make. Encourage them to draw a face that is a little different to the one you made. Then have them wash their hands before proceeding and remind them why they have to do it.

Now have the children make their faces. Put the biscuits on the Teddy Bears' plates while the icing becomes harder. If you want the children to eat the biscuits, send them to wash their hands once again and ask why they have to do that.

Follow-up

While the icing is hardening, the children could make Teddy Bear masks. Provide a bear's head template for them to trace around. You may want to make holes where the eyes are so that the children can cut them out safely.

Learning opportunities

The children can practise taking turns when talking about the picnic. They also have the chance to practise singing together. Their drawings of what they want to do with their biscuit are, in a simple way, their design plans. Encourage the children to refer to them when making their biscuits. They also begin to learn about the need for hygiene.

Fenced in

Prior experience

This activity suits more experienced children in this stage. Of course, if you or other adults support the children more closely, you could use it successfully with others.

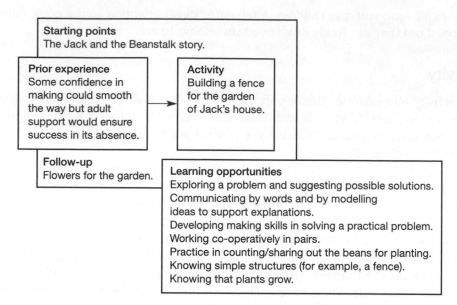

Figure 4.7 *Outline of an activity involving building a model fence for a garden.*

The Starting Point

Tell the *Jack and the Beanstalk* story from an illustrated book. Show the children some dried broad beans at the relevant point in the story to make sure they know what you are talking about.

Activity

If a toy house is available, you could use that as the background for the fences the children make. Otherwise, make a simple house from a cardboard box. Stand the house on a large sheet of green paper to represent the garden. Now show your toy or model house and have the children identify the parts. Point out that, without a fence, the cow might eat the vegetables then Jack and his mum would have nothing to eat. Ask what a fence is and what it is for. If necessary, have the children look at a fence. Ask how we might make a garden fence for Jack's house. Show what there is available (lollipop sticks or narrow strips of thick card). Let the children handle the materials. Have the children model their ideas with the materials to help them explain what they would like to do. If necessary, gently help their thinking towards what is likely to be successful. Take the fences that they make and fix them around the garden.

Follow-up

Draw attention to the garden. It is fenced in now but nothing is growing in it. Have ready a piece of thick string with paper leaves attached along its length to represent the beanstalk. Use adhesive tape to fasten one end to a spot in the garden. Attach a length of thread to the other end and use the thread to make the beanstalk slowly grow. Retell the story briefly as you do so, inviting the children to tell you what happens next. Take the beans that you showed the children earlier and show them how to plant them in pots of damp compost. In pairs, have them plant two beans in a pot. You might like to have 'one you prepared earlier' to show the children. They can then observe the growth of the pre-prepared one while they wait for their beans to grow.

Learning opportunities

This activity provides an opportunity for the children to talk about a problem (how to make a fence) and tell you and others about ideas they have. The children can exercise choice and demonstrate what they will make. In the process, they construct a simple structure to solve a practical problem. The follow-up work provides a chance to learn about plants and is an opportunity for some simple number work.

D&T-related activities in outline for the 3 – 5 stage

Using paper and card

Stamps for letters

Prior experience: This involves using safe scissors and suits a wide range of children.

Starting points: Talk about sending and receiving birthday cards and the need for an envelope and a stamp. Pass some used envelopes around for the children to examine.

Activity: Give the children a piece of paper or card that will fit into an envelope. Have them draw a picture for a parent or carer. Provide an envelope. Now they must make a stamp for the envelope. From the examples of stamps on the used envelopes, have the children design and make their own stamps and attach them to the envelope.

Paper chains

Prior experience: The skills needed are not demanding (cutting paper strips and gluing) so the activity will suit a range of ages and experiences.

Starting points: The need for paper chains could come from an event (for example, to welcome a new member of the class, Hawaiian style, or to decorate a tree or birthday display).

Activity: Have the children examine a variety of coloured papers (such as those used for wrapping gifts). Show them how to make loops and interlock them to make a chain. Have them tell you what is wrong with making a pile of glued loops to make into a chain later.

Place mats

Prior experience: Children should be able to grasp the nature of the problem: we do not want the plates and saucers to scratch the table. The skills are not demanding (cutting folded paper with scissors) so the activity will suit a wide range of children.

Starting points: Adjust a story slightly to have a character scratch the table with a plate (for example, *Goldilocks and the Three Bears*: 'Who's been eating my porridge – and' (gasp!) 'scratched the table with my bowl!').

Activity: Ask how we might stop a plate scratching a table. Show the children some examples of place mats. Offer a range of papers to choose from. Ask which would be the best to make a place mat and ask why. Show the children how to make a pattern in the paper by folding it before cutting it. Let them try it then make a place mat.

Napkins

Prior experience: This is suitable for any child who can grasp the nature of the problem: we do not want to drop food on our clothes.

Starting points: Sooner or later, a child will drop food on themselves and that makes a good time to introduce the activity. Alternatively, follow Place Mats with this activity.

Activity: We need some napkins that feel and look nice. Have a range of papers ready and pass them around for the children to examine. Ask which they think would make a good napkin and ask for reasons. Show the children what pinking scissors can do and have them practise with them then make a napkin. (Use children's safe, plastic, pinking scissors).

Springy zig–zags

Prior experience: The children will need to use safe scissors and adhesive tape.

Starting points: A story about caterpillars, worms or snakes (for example, the ever popular, *The Very Hungry Caterpillar* by Eric Carle) will turn children's minds to small living things. In the right season, you may be able to take the children to see caterpillars on garden plants.

Activity: Have the children make a caterpillar (or worm or snake) by cutting a strip of paper which they colour and fold in a zig-zag fashion. They attach this to a small ball (for example, a ping pong ball) using adhesive tape (see figure 4.8). The ball is the caterpillar's head. Eyes may be added using circles of coloured adhesive paper. (The same approach can be used to make arms, legs or tails for animals with paper bodies. It also provides an opportunity to develop descriptive vocabulary, such as, springy, stretchy, bouncy.)

Figure 4.8 *A caterpillar.*

Calling cards

Prior experience: The children need to understand that their names can be represented on paper using letters.

Starting points: A need for name labels occurs fairly often in the classroom (for example, on tables, on belongings, in cloakrooms). Take the opportunity as the need arises.

Activity: With the children watching, type in their names in a sans serif font in bold using the computer. If possible, let the children choose an item of clip art and you paste it next to their names for them. Print out several copies of the names on thin card and cut them out to give to the children. Remind the children that it is easy to lose name cards. How will they solve the problem? One way is to store the cards in envelopes. You could have the children decorate the envelopes in a variety of ways. Another way is to have the children punch a single hole in the end of each card and thread them onto a treasury tag.

A tidy cupboard

Prior experience: The children need to be able to fold thin card to make edges meet.

Starting points: You will want to develop the habit of tidiness in the children. For example, in the toy cupboard, everything has its place.

Activity: Give the children an A4 sheet of card. Have them fold it so that the outer edges meet in the middle (figure 4.9). The children open the card again and, on

the central part, draw shelves and pictures of toys arranged tidily on the shelves. The two flaps become doors for the cupboard by inserting a paper fastener in each as handles. (With older children, you could have them make a 'cupboard' from a cereal packet by cutting flap-like doors in the front.)

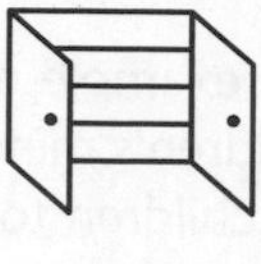

Figure 4.9 *Folded card to make a 'cupboard'.*

Turning Wheels: Weather indicator and merry-go-round

Prior experience: These activities involve the use of safe scissors and are generally suited to a wide range of young children.

Starting points: Have the children explore wheels. How many can they find? How do they work? What are they used for?

Activity: Have the children draw around a large lid to make a circle on card. They cut out the circle and, using a drawing pin, fix it to a block of wood or piece of fibre board so that the card turns freely about its centre. The next step is to make this into a: 'What is the Weather Today?' disc. A pointer is drawn on the rotatable disc and a sun, a cloud, rain and snow are drawn on the base board around the disc. You could take this further with another disc. The children cut-out animals to attach to the outer edge of the card circle. Show them how to leave a tab at the base of each figure, bend it at a right angle and use that to glue the figure upright on the card circle. The children can turn the merry-go-round using finger tips.

Waste bin

Prior experience: The children need to cut moderately thick card in this activity.

Starting points: As part of your 'being tidy' campaign (see above), you could tell the children a Womble story.

Activity: Have the children do a room Womble and collect all the things that should be put away. They will need a waste bin for litter. Ask them what they might use. Can they make one? Help them use safety snips to make a waste bin from a cardboard box.

Crown it all

Prior experience: This crown is a circle of card that will fit a child's head. If you help the children get the size right when making the circle, a wide range of children can do this activity.

Starting points: Many traditional fairy tales involve kings, queens, princes or princesses. Associated pictures show them wearing crowns. Use one to lead to the activity.

Activity: Make a crown beforehand by cutting a broad strip of card from an A3 sheet and cutting 'teeth' along one of the long edges. Fix it in a circle using adhesive tape. Before you show the children your crown, have them examine crowns in pictures. Ask how they would make a crown and what they would use. Show them your crown and ask them how you made it. Have them make a crown and decorate it with 'jewels' made from coloured sweet paper and foils.

A Clock

Prior experience: The children should be able to cut to a line using safe scissors. You could use the activity to introduce clocks and time but the children do not have to be able to tell the time.

Starting points: Have the children learn and recite the nursery rhyme, *Hickory, Dickory, Dock, The mouse ran up the clock*. Use this to introduce the clock-making activity.

Activity: Draw circles for clock faces on A4 pieces of card beforehand. Have the children cut out the circles. (If they can, you could have them copy the numbers in their correct places on their clock dials with the help of a real clock.) Using card of a contrasting colour, have the children make pointers. Punch a hole in one end of each pointer. Help the child locate the centre of the clock dial and make a hole there. Fix the pointers in place using a paper fastener. (Open the fastener slightly for the child and ensure it is used safely.) At different times in the day, have the child reset the clock to match the position of the pointers on a real clock.

Animals

Prior experience: This involves making holes in shoe boxes to fit card tubes. You start the holes yourself and the children will enlarge them to suit the tube size. The activity is suitable for older children in this stage.

Starting points: Picture books of animals and stories of pets make good starting points for this activity (for example, pets, farm animals or wild animals).

Activity: The activity develops children's awareness of structures and their properties. It also shows them that many different things can be made from the same items.

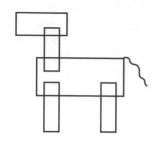

Figure 4.10 *A shoe box animal.*

Collect several shoe boxes (for example, from your local shoe shop) and kitchen roll tubes. You also need some smaller boxes and knitting wool or string. Use a shoe box as the body of the animal. Make holes near the corners on the underside of a box. Insert tubes as legs (figure 4.10). Make a hole in the top of the box for the neck. Fit a smaller box on the neck to make the head. It should be possible to turn the head so that it can 'look' at things around the room. Add a tail made from string or wool.

Using fabrics

Some activities that use paper, such as Place Mats and Napkins, may be done with felt. This provides a wider range of experience. Contrasting pieces can be attached to the felt using a fabric adhesive (although a polyvinylacetate adhesive [PVA] will often work). Sewing is not always necessary but plastic needles are available if you want children to learn to sew.

Puppets

Prior experience: Making simple puppets is a popular activity as the demands are not great. It gives both imaginative play opportunities and experience of the properties of materials. The activity suits many children in this stage.

Starting points: The scene can be set using stories that provide the opportunity for the children to play the role of one of the animals. Speech and action should be involved to make the most of the puppet.

Activity: A sock can make an expressive puppet. Its shape obviously lends itself to long, thin creatures (for example, caterpillars, snakes and giraffes) but the children's imagination can make it any animal they want it to be. Show the children how to give the puppet eyes and ears by gluing on pieces of brightly coloured felt. A development is the mitt puppet where the child's thumb becomes a puppet's arm. The glove-puppet allows for two arms but requires a little more dexterity to operate.

Rug

Prior experience: This involves cutting a fringe in felt. Most children can attempt it with safe scissors.

Starting points: House building activities are described below (*A home for an animal using building blocks* and *A housing problem*). Point out that just making a house for Eeyore or the Old Woman is not enough. Houses need other things. What do they suggest? *A tidy cupboard*, see above, is one possibility. A rug is another.

Activity: If necessary, have the children practise making a fringed rug using card then they can make a 'real' rug using a rectangle of felt. The rug may be made more attractive by gluing brightly coloured pieces of felt to it. The children could also make curtains in a similar way. The problem for them is how to attach them to the windows.

Some clothes for Teddy

Prior experience: This involves cutting felt with safe scissors and applying items to it. The level of difficulty depends on the chosen item of clothing.

Starting points: The children should feel fabrics and sort them. For instance, clothing could be sorted into 'feels rough' and 'feels smooth', 'keeps you warm' and 'keeps you cool', 'keeps the rain out' and 'lets the rain in'. After this, read a Paddington Bear story to set the scene. Tell the children that he is going away for the day. Ask what he should take with him. What if it is cold and windy? What if it is hot? What if it rains?

Activity: Guide the children towards thoughts of things that they might make successfully, with a little guidance from you, such as a scarf. A real Teddy Bear will help the children focus their thoughts.

Using food

When dealing with food, always consider hygiene. Antibacterial sprays will help to ensure that surfaces are safe. You will find that disposable table covers are useful. Have the children practise their hygiene skills through, for instance, hand washing. Provide only implements and receptacles that the children can use safely. Avoid glassware and sharp items. This means that some processing will have to be done by you for the children. Do not let children have access to electrical or heating devices of any kind. After an activity, you will often want the children to help clear things away but ensure that there is no hazard in doing so. Check with parents for any food allergies (for example, to nuts and particular fruits) and bear in mind cultural and religious differences in what is acceptable to eat.

Paper plate party

Prior experience: Most children can attempt this as it involves using only safe scissors. This activity does not use real food. It is an opportunity for children to name items of food and to see its variety. They can also learn conventions for presenting and eating food.

Starting points: A story about a party, picnic or special meal would set the scene.

Activity: Have the children examine and talk about pictures of food (for example, from cookery magazines). Give them paper plates and have them make a meal on the plate by cutting out items of food from the pictures. You could also remind them of the need for cutlery and have them cut out a knife, fork and spoon from card and set the table.

Juices

Prior experience: This activity involves choices and mixing juices to make a new taste. Most children can be involved in this. Help older children to consider unequal quantities of the juices – a dash of this and a lot of that may make a nice drink. Remember to check for food allergies.

Starting points: The Teddy Bears' Picnic can be used to introduce the activity. 'What should they take to drink?' The nursery rhyme, *Polly Put the Kettle On* could also be a starting point. You might follow it with, 'I don't like tea. What do you like to drink?'

Activity: Have some cartons of juice ready (for example, grapefruit, orange, peach, tomato, mixed fruit). Which drink do you like? Using a disposable plastic cup for each child, have them taste a little of the fruit drinks and rank them according to preference. Introduce the mixed fruit drink. Could they make a better one? What would they use? What would they do? Have them try it.

Fruit salad (using ready-chopped fruit)

Prior experience: In some respects, this is a variation of the juices activity but, here, the emphasis is on presentation. Most children can be involved. Remember to check for food allergies.

Starting points: The Teddy Bears' Picnic can be used to introduce the activity: 'What is nice to eat on a hot day?' An alternative would be the celebration of a birthday.

Activity: Show the children an orange then peel and segment it into a bowl. Repeat this with a grapefruit into another bowl, asking them to predict what it will be like. Do the same for other fruit (avoiding fruits that go brown on standing). Explain what a mixed fruit salad is. Give the children circles of paper and have them draw their ideas for a fruit salad. Follow this with plastic bowls and have the children 'make' their designs by collecting fruit with tongs or a large spoon and arranging it without touching it in the bowls. They could then set the table for a fruit salad meal.

Grow your own

Prior experience: There are no great demands on skills or formal knowledge so this is suitable for a wide range of children. Remember to check for food allergies.

Starting points: Rabbit in *Winnie the Pooh* books grows his own food in his garden. Can they do the same?

Activity: You need some seeds that sprout readily (for example, alfalfa or mung bean – use those intended for sprouting and eating and not those for sowing in the garden: the latter may have been chemically treated). Soak the seeds for one or two hours before you need them. Rinse and drain the seeds. Have the children put a spoonful of the soaked seeds in a transparent pot and cover the top with a piece of thin cloth. Each day, rinse the seeds with fresh water and drain off the excess. Have the children watch them sprout.

Food for the birds

Prior experience: This activity is intended to help children see similarities and differences between our needs and those of other animals. This is something for the older children.

Starting points: Have the children watch the birds. Focus their attention on them using questions (for example, How many are there? Are they all the same? What are they doing? What are they looking for? Do we have anything they might eat? Could we make a meal for them?).

Activity: Providing a meal for the birds is the problem. What will they eat? What have we got? Should we mix it up or keep the things separate? How big should the bits be? Where should we put the food? Provide a range of things for the children to choose from (for example, bread, a carrot, a chocolate sweet, nuts, peas, cake, biscuits, apple). The children can cut these using safe scissors and watch the birds eat. Afterwards, have the children see what the birds did not eat.

Using clay

Clay pennies

Prior experience: The level of skill needed is not great but it is better to do this activity with those who grasp that pennies are used to buy things. The children do not have to use them in the correct combination. They can treat them more as tokens. It can, however, give them practice at counting and exchanging their clay coins for goods.

Starting points: Set up a shop corner. This introduces the need for coins.

Activity: Using a clay that does not need to be fired, show the children how to roll out a relatively thin sheet of clay. Using a tube with a circular cross-section that is roughly the size of a coin, have them press out discs of clay. If necessary, remove the discs from the tube gently using a piece of wood. Allow the discs to harden then have the children paint them.

Pencil–Stand

Prior experience: This is suitable for a wide range of children. Self-hardening clay is used to make a solid shape with at least one flat face.

Starting points: Remind the children of Humpty Dumpty. Show them a ball made to look like Humpty Dumpty. Ask why he rolls off the table so easily. Ask what shape would be better for Humpty so that he would not roll off the table.

Activity: If necessary, show the children how to roll a ball of clay and give it a smooth, spherical surface. Have them make Humpty Dumpty with a flat 'bottom' so he will not fall off the table. Ask if we can use Humpty as a place to put a pencil.

Use a pencil to make a deep hole. Have the children make Humpty into a pencil-stand and let it harden. They should finish them using paint.

Clay figures

Prior experience: The children have the opportunity to shape clay, use pastry cutters to press out figures and finish them in various ways. Several steps are involved so you may prefer to use the activity with older children.

Starting points: The need for simple figures often arises during the making of other things. So, for instance, the children may make a car from a small cardboard box and need someone to drive it or they may need a star to decorate a tree.

Activity: Using a clay that does not need to be fired, show the children how to roll out a thin sheet of clay and use pastry cutters to press out the shapes. These shapes can be prepared to suit their needs by bending them (so that a figure appears to be seated) or by making holes in them (so that they can be suspended). When hard, they are to be finished with paint. A coating of PVA adhesive can give them a glossy finish. Before the adhesive hardens, sand or glitter may be sprinkled on various parts of the figure.

Thumb pots

Prior experience: This task involves moulding by hand. It can be messy so appropriate protection for hands, clothing and surfaces is needed. Given that, most children can be involved in this activity.

Starting points: Show the children an egg-cup. Ask what it is and why it is shaped like that. Can they make an egg-cup? Set them the challenge.

Activity: If possible, the children should see clay dug by you using a spade. Make sure that the clay contains no sharp bits and take some indoors. Cover the tables to protect them and give the children plastic bags for their hands so that they can handle the clay. Show them how to mould small pieces into shapes. Afterwards, repeat this using a manufactured clay that hardens without firing. The children can decorate these pots by painting them. They could be tested using a hard-boiled egg. (They could, of course, make an 'egg' from clay.)

Using wood

Activities like these will add children's awareness of wood as a construction material and give them opportunities to become aware of some of its forms and properties.

Wooden toys

Prior experience: No great prior experience is needed but the children need to be interested in how things work.

Starting points: Provide some wooden toys for the children to play with and explore. These can vary from simple toys on four wheels to wooden dolls with hinged arms and legs and toys with wooden cams.

Activity: Name parts of the toys for the children (like wheels and axles, hinge, crank handle). Ask the children to tell you and the others how the toys work: 'How do the wheels turn?' 'What lets its arms move?' 'Why doesn't its head fall off?'.

Flowers for the teacher

Prior experience: There is no need for great skill or formal knowledge so a wide range of children can be involved.

Starting points: Ask how people make their houses look nice. Do some of them use flowers? Point out that you do not have flowers in the room. If each of them made a flower, they could have a vase of flowers.

Activity: The problem is how to make the flowers. By questioning, identify the parts of the flower they need to make (coloured petals and green stem). Ask what they might use for a stem. Have some lengths of wooden dowel to hand (about 25cm long). Ask if these would be useful. How could they make them green? What could they use for petals. Have some coloured tissue paper to hand and show them that it can be crumpled to make a ball. How could they fix it to the dowel? On completion, display the 'flowers' in a vase. Ensure that the children are careful when working with the dowel so that they do not poke someone (or themselves) in an eye.

Using mixed materials and components

By 'mixed materials' is meant recycled (reclaimed) materials, such as, cereal boxes, coffee jar lids, plastic pop bottles and kitchen roll tubes and other construction materials, such as, fabrics, clay and strip wood. It also includes ready-made components, such as, wheels and pulleys (or bobbins) and simple kits, like wooden or plastic blocks.

A home for an animal using building blocks

Prior experience: This introduces children to making structures using building blocks. Large blocks do not need fine manipulative skills. Commercial kits are available but a supply of cardboard boxes can do just as well. Most children in this stage can be involved in this activity.

Starting points: A story about making a home for an animal will set the scene (for example, *A New House for Eeyore*, adapted from *The House at Pooh Corner* by A.A. Milne, 1999).

Activity: Have the children make a home for an animal, such as Eeyore. They should consider what the home will have (for example, a door, a window and a roof). The roof will test many young children's problem-solving skills so be prepared to help with that.

A housing problem

Prior experience: This activity calls for the use of safety snips to make holes in a cardboard box. If you help with cutting the card, it can be attempted by a wide range of children. The older ones will generally need less support.

Starting points: One starting point is the rhyme, *The old woman who lived in a shoe*. This presents a problem to solve. How many children does she have? How many beds will she need? What else must she have? How could we make a house for her?

Activity: Here, the children use the materials around them and their imaginations to make a house with doors and windows. Provide some cardboard boxes, like those used for duplicating paper. Have the children mark out the windows and doors on a box and help them cut them out using safety snips. Ask if they can make a door that works and, if necessary, show them how to make such a door by fixing one edge in place using adhesive tape. Ask what they might use to make windows and, if necessary, show them how to fit 'glass' in a window using a small square of transparent plastic sheet. The house needs furniture. Have the children tell you what they need and let them use recycled materials for it.

A drink for the birds

Prior experience: Demands on formal knowledge are not great so this can be attempted by a wide range of children.

Starting points: Take an opportunity to have the children observe birds from the window on a dry day. This helps you introduce the problem.

Activities: Ask if birds drink water like we do. Point out that there is no water for the birds to drink. Can they do anything to help? A large dish of water would be too big; the birds might fall in it. What could we use? Where would we put it? What if it is windy? How could we stop it blowing away? If necessary, shape the children's ideas so that they stand a good chance of being successful. Let the children try some of them.

Pot pourri

Prior experience: This does not demand much in the way of formal knowledge. The children can acquire what they need by listening to and watching you.

Starting point: This is best attempted in the Autumn when there are lots of leaves around. Collect a bag of clean, dry leaves, making sure that there is nothing hazardous amongst them. On taking the children into a room, complain that it does not smell nice. This introduces the problem.

Activity: What can we do about it? If necessary, suggest that we could let fresh air into the room by opening a window. What else could we do? Let the children sniff some flowery scents produced by a drop or two of various perfumed oils on cotton wool or blotting paper (but do not let them get oil on themselves). Tell the children that the oils are expensive. We have to make a drop or two go a long way. Put some leaves into several bags. Add drops of oil to each and have the children shake the bags. Let them see that the leaves now smell of the oil. We could spread these around the room but the problem with that is that we would end up with a mess. Ask how they could have leaves around the room so that the perfume spreads out without making the room messy.

CHAPTER 5

D&T Activities for 5 – 7 Year Olds

This chapter describes D&T activities for the 5 – 7 stage, also known as Key Stage 1 in some regions. In this stage, D&T can have more subject-centred goals and may have a distinct identity. Frequently, however, you are likely to use an activity to contribute to a variety of learning goals. In other words, the teaching of distinct subjects in separate slots may evolve in this stage or be left to the next stage. Nevertheless, D&T activities need to be planned, organized and purposeful. Maintain progress and prevent a build up of frustrated effort by judicious support. The amount and kind of support should be tailored to the capabilities of the child but do not take all the challenge out of the task and do not provide too many detailed, step-by-step instructions that remove opportunities for creativity. As in the earlier stage, you may have adult helpers. If so, they need to be clear about the purpose of an activity and what is expected of them.

Examples

Some examples of D&T-centred activities follow. The time needed for each is indicated approximately in terms of sessions of about one hour duration. Of course, you can digress, omit an activity or add others, according to the needs of your children. The *Contexts* suggest ideas to give the activities meaning and purpose and catch the children's interest. The *Knowledge resource* blocks refer to what you may need to develop for the activities. Often, this will take place in your teaching of another subject, such as science. A *Focused activity* is the fairly structured activity intended to develop some skill, know-how or device knowledge. A focused activity is not always needed and the examples illustrate tasks with and without focused activities. As the name suggests, a *Designing and making activity* is intended to give children the opportunity to be creative. The *Closing event* suggests ways of consolidating or extending learning. Some *Learning opportunities* are also listed but these cannot be exhaustive as you could use the tasks in other ways. Note that teaching D&T is not a matter of giving the child an activity to do and letting them get on with it. It involves active teaching and involvement on your part so that the children can make the most of an activity.

After these examples is a stock of teaching ideas. These are not in the same detail as the examples but may be taught similarly. Remember that at the beginning of this stage you will have children who could still benefit from the activities listed for the earlier stage. Use them as they are or adapt them to suit the needs of such children. At the same time, some of the activities described below may offer something for older ones in the 3 – 5 stage, provided that you simplify them or support the children more closely. Stories and visits continue to be useful in providing meaningful contexts for the tasks. A Planning Sheet to help you develop such ideas, including ideas you have yourself, is provided at the end of the *Appendix*.

The problem with bags

This piece of D&T work has a fairly simple structure as it goes straight from knowledge development into a practical problem to solve. The practical skills are not demanding and can be attempted by a wide range of children. You need to set aside three sessions, one each for knowledge development, designing and making to solve the problem, and consolidation and extension.

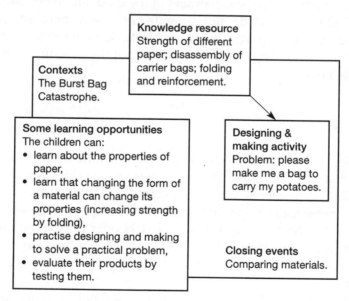

Figure 5.1 *Outline of an activity to make a 'better' paper bag.*

Knowledge resource

This could be developed in science. You could have the children examine a range of papers and describe their properties (for instance, thick, thin; see-through, not see-through; soft, hard; strong, weak). Have them put the papers in order from what they think is strong to what they think is weak. Ask how they might test the papers to see if they are correct and then try it.

Have a range of paper bags to hand. Ask the children which they think will be the strongest. What makes them strong? (For example, thick paper, double thickness paper.) How are the handles made? Where might the weak parts be? Have the children tease the bags apart to see how they are made.

Designing and making activity

Beforehand, weaken a paper bag of potatoes so that when you take your hand away, the potatoes fall out. Arrive in the room with your bag of potatoes. When you have the children's attention, lift the bag and let the potatoes fall out, as if by accident. 'Oh, dear! That always happens to me! These bags are not strong enough. Now I've got nothing to carry the potatoes in. I'll bet you could make me a bag that would work.' Have the children think about designs for a bag. Ask how they will make it strong and whether it should have a handle. Have the children make their bags and test them carefully with some potatoes.

Closing events

Collect a variety of bags (for example, a paper carrier bag, a plastic carrier bag, a net bag, a textile bag). Have some items to put in them (for instance, cans of food, nails, plastic beaker of water, fruit, a birthday gift, frozen peas). Ask the children which bag would be best for each item, taking them one-by-one. Ask for reasons for their choices. Afterwards, focus on the birthday gift and suggest that none of the bags would be very good for that. Ask what a bag for a gift should be like. Have them print patterns on paper using ICT or with potato-prints. They might then design and make a fancy gift bag for some chocolate for mum.

The problem with tall vases

This activity can stem from work on stability in science. At the outset, it involves using a construction kit to test ideas. A practical problem is then presented for the children to solve. The knowledge part might take one session and the problem-solving activity another lesson. The activities could be attempted by a wide range of children.

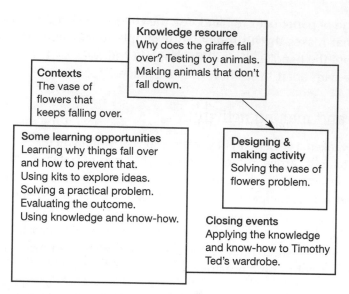

Figure 5.2 *Outline of an activity to do with making tall, narrow objects more stable.*

Knowledge resource

This could come from a science-related activity in which the children classify toy animals into those that fall over easily and those that do not. Choose toys carefully so that the set includes a variety of animal shapes and sizes. Ask, for instance, why the giraffe falls over easily but the elephant does not. Do long legs make a difference? Does having big feet make a difference? The next step is to have children test their ideas. Give them a simple construction kit to build animals. Ask them to make a giraffe that will not fall over easily. Can they also make an elephant that will fall over easily? (Children who are unfamiliar with kits often need additional play time to learn what they can do.)

Designing and making activity

Place a bunch of large, artificial flowers in a narrow vase so that it is unstable. Stand it on a table and let it fall over. Ask how the vase of flowers is like, for instance, a giraffe. Ask for ideas that will help the vase stand up and try them. (If necessary, ask if it needs a bigger foot.) Give the children a kitchen roll tube and one of the flowers and have them solve the problem.

Closing event

You could develop children's knowledge of clothes and their properties using Timothy Ted (a furry Teddy Bear). He has clothes for hot days, clothes for cold days, and clothes for rainy days. Ask the children what they think his cold day clothes are like and what makes them warm. Continue through the other days in a similar way (see also Chapter 7 if you want to present this through a story). Of course, Timothy Ted needs a wardrobe for his clothes. Have the children make a wardrobe for Timothy from a cereal packet. Using safe scissors, doors are cut into one of the large sides. A piece of dowel makes a rail for clothes to hang on. Craft wire can be used to make coat hangers but you will need to cut the wire to length for the children and show them a real coat hanger as a model. The problem with the wardrobe is that it falls over easily. Ask the children to solve the problem.

Wheels that work

This example includes a focused activity to show the children an easy way of making axle supports. This has its own context. It is followed by a designing and making activity that gives the children the opportunity to use this know-how in a different context. The practical, manipulative and designing skills are moderately demanding so the tasks are suitable for more adept children in this stage. Safe scissors and safety snips are needed. You might begin the science-related work in one session then have the children do the focused activity in another. The designing and making activity would need another session and the closing events would add at least one more.

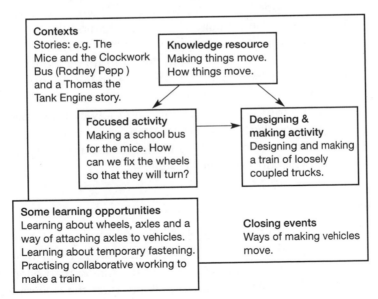

Figure 5.3 *Outline of an activity to do with making a buggy with working wheels.*

Knowledge resource

You would probably develop relevant knowledge in science-related activities, as when you use simple wheeled toys to explore what makes things move, go slower and go faster by having the toys run up and down steep and shallow slopes. Talk about the moving parts of the toys (wheels and axles).

Focused activity

Read a story, such as, *The Mice and the Clockwork Bus* by Rodney Peppé. Pause at the point where there is the need for a new bus to take the mice to school. Show the children how to make a 'bus' from a strip of wood (like a ruler) with two Bulldog clips for axle supports (figure 5.4). Stiff card could be used instead of a ruler. Have the children draw and cut out mice passengers to glue to the bus.

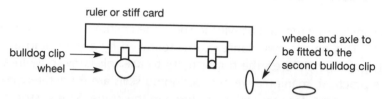

Figure 5.4 *How to make a simple bus with wheels that turn.*

Designing and making activity

Let the children watch or hear a train story (perhaps a *Thomas the Tank Engine* story by W. Awdry). Talk about making a train. If necessary, remind them of the bus they made. Make the engine yourself in the same way, cutting out the shape from stiff card or the soft plastic of an ice-cream carton. Point out that it would take too long if they all had to make a full train each. Ask what they might do instead (for example, they could each make one truck). Have them draw the truck they will make and then make it. Line up the trucks behind the train and show that they need to be fastened loosely together (coupled). Have the children solve the problem and make a train they can pull along a table top. They could, for instance, use treasury tags, paper clips or even short lengths of adhesive tape.

Closing events

You could develop the scientific knowledge further by having the children explore the use of gravity to move the bus. Have them fasten a thread to the front of the bus and a piece of modelling clay to the other end of the thread then hang the thread over the edge of a table so that it pulls the bus along. Have the children explore the effect of:

- different amounts of clay;
- tying two buses together.

Pirates' treasure

Pirates' treasure includes a focused activity to give the children some practical know-how which they can apply in the designing and making activity. If the children can grasp the context, all but the least experienced could attempt the tasks. They involve the use of safety snips or, if the card is thin, safe scissors. Allow a session for the focused activity, one for the designing and making activity and one for the follow-up work.

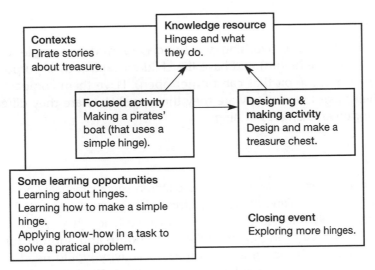

Figure 5.5 *Outline of activities that involve simple hinges.*

Knowledge resource

On this occasion, the knowledge resource is extended during and after the making activities, when the children grasp the nature of a simple hinge (see *Closing event*).

Focused activity

Remind the children that pirates need a boat so they can get from the ship to the treasure island. To make 'boats', collect shoe boxes from your local shoe shop. Give each a mast made by putting a piece of modelling clay in the centre of the box and pressing a pencil in it, point first. Make a sail from thick paper. Punch a hole in the middle of the top edge and one in the middle of the bottom edge of the paper. Slide the pencil through the holes to attach the sail. Point out that the boat sides are very high. Ask how the pirates are going to get out of the boat. Guide them to think about making a hinged flap. Show the children how to cut out a section of one end of the box and re-attach it using adhesive tape to make a drop-down end. Afterwards, draw attention to the way water may get in if the flap drops down when the boat is in deep water. Ask how they will keep the flap in place. Take suggestions and help them develop ideas.

Designing and making activity

The pirates need a treasure chest. Have the children select a box and make items of treasure from gold and silver foil and coloured paper. Ask how they will make a lid that works. Have the children solve the problem.

Closing event

Draw attention to one or two hinges in the classroom (for example, door hinges, box hinges, spectacle hinges) and have the children explain their purpose (to make a 'floppy' part or loose bit that can turn or open). Have them compare these with the way their hinges work. How are they the same? How are they different? Have them look for other examples of hinges.

In a flash

The focused activity in *In a flash* gives the children some practical know-how to use in the designing and making activity. Electrical circuits are commonly introduced to older children in this stage so these activities would follow that. Allow two sessions for the focused activity (one for modelling the house and another for fitting the torch bulb circuit). The designing and making activity would need a session for making the beacon and a session for making the street. The follow-up activity would need another session.

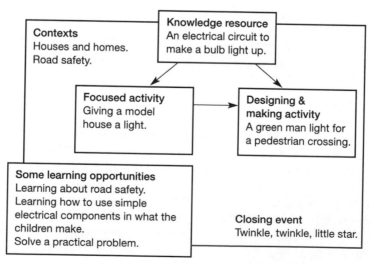

Figure 5.6 *Outline of activities involving electrical circuits.*

Knowledge resource

Begin with some science-related activities about what is needed to make a torch bulb light up. In the interests of safety, emphasize that the mains electricity is different and dangerous and that the children must have nothing to do with it.

Focused activity

Have the children make a model house from a cardboard box and have them fit a working light using a torch bulb, battery and connecting wires.

Designing and making activity

Talk about road safety. Draw attention to the red and green man at a road crossing. Ask what they are for. Can they make a green man like that? What would they need? With components in front of them, help them explore and clarify their ideas and have them draw and label what they will make. Now they need to make a street and crossing place. Again, have them draw what it will look like and then make it. You will probably need some boxes for houses and paper for the children to mark on the street and zebra-crossing.

Closing event

Use the nursery rhyme, *Twinkle, twinkle, little star*, to introduce the idea of making a star that will twinkle (flash on and off) using a simple circuit and a switch. Have the children make one.

D&T activities in outline for the 5 – 7 stage

Using paper and card

Bookmarks

This involves using safe scissors and suits a wide range of children. One session is needed. There are opportunities to explore a need and practise cutting skills when solving the problem.

Designing and making activity: When you read a story to the children, close the book as though inadvertently. Complain about having lost your place. Ask what you might do so it does not happen again. Show a range of book marks and demonstrate how they are used. Have the children design and make one for their books. Each bookmark should have the maker's name on it.

Closing event: Show the children a parcel tag with its string through a hole. Have the children work out how to make some of their own. Add labels to objects in the room, such as flowers.

Finger puppets

This involves using safe scissors and suits a wide range of children. One session is needed. The activities practise cutting and hole-making skills in paper and adapting an idea to suit a slightly different purpose.

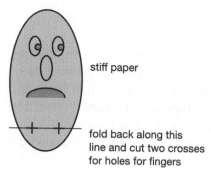

stiff paper

fold back along this line and cut two crosses for holes for fingers

Figure 5.7 *A paper puppet.*

Focused activity: Remind children of Humpty Dumpty. Show the children how to make a thin card model of Humpty (figure 5.7). The holes should be big enough for children to put their first two fingers through to use as legs.

Designing and making activity: Now tell the children a story and have them draw and make a figure for each hand to accompany the story.

Closing event: Ask how they would make an animal with four legs. Have them describe their ideas.

Hats

These activities are more demanding than those above and suit older children in this stage. It is an opportunity for children to practise following you step-by-step and to develop folding and fixing skills. Allow about two sessions.

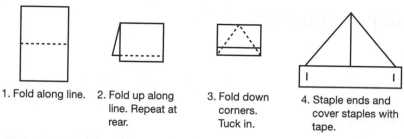

1. Fold along line.
2. Fold up along line. Repeat at rear.
3. Fold down corners. Tuck in.
4. Staple ends and cover staples with tape.

Figure 5.8 *Making a pirate's hat.*

Focused activity: Begin with a pirate story (as in *Peter Pan*). Draw attention to pirates' hats. Fold an A3 sheet of paper in half (figure 5.8). Fold up about 2cm of the ends of the paper (the amount is not crucial). Fold down the corners to make a point at the top of the hat and tuck in the folded pieces. Staple the ends and cover the staples with adhesive tape.

Designing and making activity: Talk of special hats (for instance, police hats, Robin Hood's feathered hat, hats with peaks). Have the children convert the pirate's hat into one of these (for example, by adding a badge made from card).

Closing event: Talk to the children about why it is a good idea to wear a hat on sunny days in summer.

Picture frame

This involves using safety snips and fixing skills. It provides an opportunity for children to adjust a product, decide what parts are not needed and remove them. Allow a session for the activities.

Focused activity: Use an event, such as Mother's Day, to give purpose to the activity. Have the children bring a picture of themselves. Have them cut four strips of coloured card and 'frame' the picture loosely by arranging the strips on the photograph. When they have them set up as they would like them, show them how to mark the card with a pencil and snip off the excess (figure 5.9). The children then glue the strips of card together, decorate it and attach the picture.

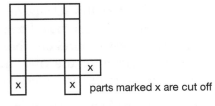

Figure 5.9 *Making a picture frame.*

Designing and making activity: Show children that pictures are often hung by a cord. Ask how they might do that. (They could make a loop from embroidery thread and attach it to the back of the frame using adhesive tape.)

Closing event: Apply what the children have learned to frame a piece of their art work.

Pencil pot and Rapunzel's Tower

This involves working with tubes, such as those in kitchen paper rolls. It gives the children an opportunity to develop cutting and fixing skills with curved surfaces. Allow a session for the focused activity (pencil pot) and another for the designing and making activity (Rapunzel's Tower).

Focused activity: Contrive a situation where there are pencils scattered around and point to the need for something to store them tidily. Suggest that a tube would make a pencil pot but show that it falls over easily and has nothing to stop the pencils from falling through. Guide the discussion towards gluing a plastic lid (for example, from a coffee jar) to the base of the tube. This gives it stability and seals the base. Help the children think of novel ways of finishing the tube.

Designing and making activity: Read the *Rapunzel* story. Clarify the meaning of 'tower' using pictures. Ask the children to design and make a tower for Rapunzel. How will they make it tower-like? How will they make Rapunzel?

Closing event: A card figure of a prince can be made to climb the tower by attaching it to one end of some ribbon and passing the other end through a window near the top of the tower. When the free end is pulled, the prince will 'climb' to the window.

TV

This practises working with thicker card and suits a wide range of children in this stage. Card is more difficult to cut than thick paper but safety snips take some of the effort out of it. Allow up to two sessions for the tasks.

Focused activity: After the children have watched a favourite programme on the television, introduce this activity. Ask them to describe a television. The television may be made from a cardboard box, like those used for duplicating paper. Have them draw the key features on a box. Where the screen is to be, make a starter hole so that the children can use safety snips to cut-out the 'screen'. Bottle top 'switches' can be attached to the box using double-sided adhesive tape.

Designing and making activity: Have the children draw pictures of animals on card and cut them out. These are to perform in the television. Ask how they will make that happen. (For example, they could glue the animal shapes to long strips of rigid card and insert them through a hole in the side or suspend figures by threads from holes in the top of the 'TV').

Closing event: Use a sheet of greaseproof paper to cover the hole where the screen is. Shine a torch from the back of the TV to cast shadows of the children's figures onto the greaseproof paper. Have the children use the figures as shadow-puppets.

Money box

This practises cutting a more difficult shape in card and needs persistence and care. The task is meaningful for a wide range of children. Allow one session.

Designing and making activity: Show the children several different money boxes. Draw attention to the slot and to the means of extracting the money when it is needed. Ask if they could make a money box. Remind them that it does not have to look like the ones you showed them but it should have a slot for the money to go in and a way of getting it out again. Invite them to look at the store of recycled materials to see if that gives them ideas. Have them explain the ideas to the rest and try them out. For safety, help the children start the making of the slot.

Closing event: Examine a postbox and discuss what it is and what it does.

Jack and Jill's Well and Swing

These activities involve the use of safety snips. The focused activity needs one session. The next activity may take more than one session to complete. It is a fairly demanding task and is better suited to more dextrous children.

Knowledge resource: Many children will not know what a well is so show them pictures and explain what wells are.

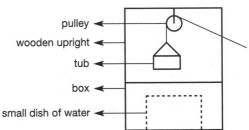

Focused activity: Remind children of the *Jack and Jill* nursery rhyme. The aim is to construct a fairly large 'well' that works. Have the children help you solve the many small 'problems'

Figure 5.10 *A well.*

involved in building the well. You need a stout cardboard box, some lengths of strip wood, a simple pulley (or bobbin), some string and a circular plastic tub (for example, a margarine tub). If necessary, cut the wood into three lengths to suit the box (figure 5.10). Two are glued to the box. The other is glued across the top. Suspend the pulley from the one across the top using string. Fasten the plastic tub to one end of the string and thread the free end through the pulley. To make it more realistic, you could put a small dish of water in the box.

Knowledge resource: A playground visit or picture will remind children of swings and their supporting structure.

Designing and making activity: Discuss how the children might make a swing, drawing on the making of the well for ideas. Provide the children with boxes (for example, from your local shoe shop). You could have them cut two equal strips of card from the box

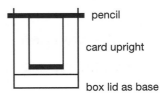

Figure 5.11 *A swing.*

and make a hole in one end of each strip using a paper punch. These strips are glued to a shoe box lid to make uprights for the swing. The holes should be at the top. Attach lengths of thread to a pencil for the children and fit the pencil into the holes in the uprights. Ask the children where the seat should be. What could they use to make a seat? Let them solve the problem and attach the seat to the dangling threads using PVA adhesive (figure 5.11).

Closing event: Talk with the children about the 'up-and-over' shapes they have been making. Show a picture of an arch in a garden catalogue. Ask them to find other shapes like that (for example, door frame, window, table).

A Car for Teddy

Children often find making wheels that work on buggies quite difficult. This shows one way that is within the grasp of a wide range of children. Safety snips are used.

Knowledge resource: Have the children examine toys with wheels and explain how the wheels are fitted and what makes it possible for them to turn. (Some toys have transparent bodies with moving parts in different colours. This supports description and explanation.)

Designing and making activity: Any of the many toy and animal stories involving buggies will provide a context for the activity (for example, *Busytown Race Day*, by Richard Scarry). You will need boxes (for example, shoe boxes) for the children to make a buggy. Show the children a shoe box and ask them if they could make a car for Teddy from it. Have them talk about what the car might look like and how they would shape the box. Introduce the problem of fitting ready-made wheels. Show the children how to use a pencil to make holes in the box and fit a ready-cut axle (wooden dowel) and wheels. Point out the need to have the axles parallel to the box ends. They should draw a picture of what they would like to make and then make it. Ensure that holes are made safely and have the children use their pictures to explain what they are doing and why.

Closing event: Have the children test the buggies by rolling them down a slope. Did the wheels turn properly? If not, why not? What might make it work better? What might make it look better?

Up and Away: aeroplanes

In this activity, the children learn to make an axle support (see also *Wheels that work* in the examples). This is better suited to more experienced children.

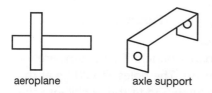

aeroplane   axle support

Figure 5.12 *Aeroplane parts.*

Knowledge resource: Name the external parts of an aeroplane and have the children practise using the words.

Designing and making activity: Use one of the many stories of aeroplanes to provide a context (for example, *Nobody Owns the Sky: The story of Brave Bessie Coleman* by R. Lindbergh). While the children watch, begin to assemble a simple aeroplane. Glue two matching strips of card together to make the body and wings (figure 5.12). Ask how we might attach its wheels. Guide the children to think about making an axle support and collect their ideas. (Figure 5.11 shows one made from a strip of card with holes punched in the ends.) Have the children try out their axle supports and evaluate them.

Closing event: Drawing on their experience, discuss what makes a good axle support.

Scissors and the Picker–Upper

This introduces pivots and is well-suited to older children in this stage. As described, allow three sessions. If you feel that the children are up to it, you could go straight to the designing and making activity and introduce the problem. After that, you could talk about scissor-action and sow the seeds of a solution. This would probably take two sessions.

Knowledge resource: Examine a pair of safe scissors with the children and describe the parts.

Focused activity: Have the children make a pair of scissors from card, using a paper fastener for the pivot.

Designing and making activity: Flik is a worker ant and a bit of an inventor. Worker ants pick up food all day and take it to the ants' nest. Flik wants to invent a picker-upper to make life easier for the worker ants (*Flik the Inventor* by Victoria Saxon). Ask the children if they can help Flik. Can they invent a picker-upper for him? If necessary, have the children think about the scissors they made. Would a giant pair of scissors do the trick?

Closing event: When the children have made a scissor-action picker-upper, ask if it picks up everything. What does it not pick up? Can they improve it to make it pick up more things? You could have the children make a scissor-action crocodile with teeth (figure 5.13).

Figure 5.13 *A crocodile picker-upper.*

Using fabrics

A purse

These activities introduce joining by sewing. They are suited to those children who can handle a large sewing needle safely. They will need at least two sessions, depending on the nature of follow-up work.

Focused activity: When you introduce the concept of money to the children using, for example, plastic coins, point out that they may lose the coins. Show a variety of purses. Have the children examine them to see how they are made. Give each child a piece of card (about 10cm by 20cm). Show how to fold it in half and sew down the sides using, for example, an overstitch in button thread or a bright embroidery thread. Leave the top edge open to slide in 'coins'.

Designing and making activity: Let each child choose a rectangle of coloured felt (pre-cut to about 10cm by 20cm). Ask them how they might make it into a purse for their money.

Closing event: Purses can be personalized using shapes cut from contrasting scraps of felt. Purses also need a means of holding them closed. One solution is to use a Bulldog clip. Another is to sew on a button and make a slit in the felt on the opposite side to feed the button through.

Weaving: Making a rug for a model house

These activities help children understand the woven nature of some cloths and practise the process of weaving. It needs about two sessions.

Knowledge resource: Let the children examine textile scraps closely and tease out the threads. Have them see the way the threads are woven together.

Focused activity: Have the children cut strips of coloured paper and weave them together to make a paper rug.

Designing and making activity: Have the children cut narrow strips of felt and make a rug, as above. Ask how they will stop the rug falling to pieces, like the scraps of textile they examined. (They could, for instance, glue a backing on it.)

Closing event: Using boxes as model houses, if necessary, display the children's rugs and have them comment on their function and appearance.

Using food

Foodstuffs are not like other materials. They must be processed hygienically, they must be stored appropriately and be fit for consumption. These needs should be discussed with the children and suitable attitudes and practices regarding hygiene and processing should be fostered. Children usually have likes and dislikes, some founded on experience and some not. It can be counter-productive to press children to taste things they do not want to taste. Often, the best approach is not to make it an issue but simply set an example by tasting things yourself and being honest about the taste. Remember, too, that some foodstuffs can be unfamiliar to some children and avoid offending social and religious practices. Be aware that some foodstuffs, such as nuts, can cause dangerous allergic responses and should be avoided. Some fruits can also produce an allergic response. Check for allergies with parents.

Yoghurts

This helps children learn that mixing foodstuffs can alter their properties (taste, texture, appearance). An extended session will allow time for all the tasks and make the most of the fresh produce.

Focused activity: Show the children some natural yoghurt and a fruit yoghurt. Have them compare their colour, texture and taste. Ask how the second yoghurt got its taste. What is in it? Can they make the first into the second? Provide some fruit. Show the children how to crush them with a fork and incorporate them in natural yoghurt. Have them taste and evaluate their product.

Designing and making activity: Challenge the children to make 'The Best-Ever Yoghurt'. Provide natural yoghurt and various fruits, cut into small pieces. Avoid those that go brown in air, like apple. Have the children evaluate their product.

Closing event: Talk about the need to keep food, such as yoghurt, fit to eat. Explain that keeping it cold helps to keep it fit to eat, hence the refrigerator.

Sundaes

The activity shows children that mixing things can change their taste and appearance. This task uses a mechanical (crank-operated) whisk. For convenience, you could do both tasks in an extended session.

Knowledge resource: Develop the children's knowledge of the origins of common foodstuffs. Where do they come from?

Focused activity: You need a carton of fresh, cold milk and some powdered dessert mixes (for example, Angel Delight®). Let the children examine the ingredients. Demonstrate how to make the dessert. Using small, safe, mixing bowls and a mechanical whisk, each child (or pair) is to make a small amount of the dessert. Work out how much milk they need and share the powders accordingly. You could either put the correct amount of milk in the bowls for the children or provide a plastic measuring jug with the correct level marked for them to use. After whisking, they could transfer the mix to plastic bowls and sprinkle it with vermicelli or hundreds and thousands. Wafers could be added. If a refrigerator is available, the dessert may be chilled.

Designing and making activity: This draws on what has been learned in the yoghurt activities. Provide a variety of chopped fruit and invite the children to design and make a fruit sundae.

Closing event: Talk about dental hygiene, why we should keep our teeth clean and avoid too many sugary things.

Bread and sandwiches

Bread-making is a popular, teacher-led activity in this stage. While the bread is baking, you can have the children explore some of its uses. The tasks could extend over three sessions, if you wish.

Knowledge resource: Show the children a loaf of bread, some flour and some wheat. Have them grind some wheat in a mortar and pestle to make 'flour'. Establish the sequence, wheat into flour into bread.

Focused activity: Show the children how to make some dough. Have each child (or pair) make a bun-sized piece. Either, proof the dough in the usual way and bake it in an oven for the children (you having complete control of everything and anything to do with the oven) or use a bread-making machine to do it for you (again, you having complete control of it, for safety).

Focused activity: Open a fresh pack of sandwiches that have a mixed filling. Ask the children why the container is shaped as it is. Let them sniff a closed sandwich and ask them what they think will be in it. Open a sandwich and, together, sort out and name the components of the filling.

Designing and making activity: Provide a wide range of chopped food items in covered dishes (for example, tomato, pepper, grated cheese) and slices of bread and spread. Have the children look at what is available and draw a picture of the sandwich they would like to make. Let them make and evaluate the sandwich. (Use only safe cutlery, such as spoons.)

Closing event: When the bread is cool, cut slices and compare it with the bread the children have used for sandwiches. If you have a supply of ripe autumn fruits, you could line a bowl with thin slices of the bread and fill it with the fruit. When the bread is soaked in fruit juice, the children could be invited to taste the 'bread pudding'.

Using clay

Clay is an example of a malleable material that can be used to solve some practical problems. Natural clay, when damp, can be worked into shapes and fired to make bricks and pots. When mixed with one or more oils, it makes a popular modelling material for children (such as modelling clay). Many schools do not have access to a kiln to fire natural clay but artificial 'clays' are available that can be hardened with gentle heat or by leaving it for a few hours. Not all clay products need to be fired.

Coaster and Pot

This is suitable for a wide range of children. It involves rolling clay to an even thickness and cutting it into a regular shape. Allow at least two sessions.

Knowledge resource: Some work on the properties of clay in science-related activities would be relevant but is not essential. Allow two sessions and additional time for painting.

Focused activity: Show the children cup ring marks on tables and have them deduce their cause. Let them try to rub them off and show that prevention is better than cure. Ask how the marks might be prevented. Show the children how to roll out and cut clay into regular shapes larger than the base of a mug. Leave the shapes to harden and have the children finish them with paint and give them a glossy coating with PVA adhesive. The children could gift-wrap their coasters.

Designing and making activity: Show that a teapot may also mark a table. Show some teapot-stands. Have the children design and make a teapot-stand.

Closing event: The children can make small slab pots by rolling out clay, cutting sides and a base, dampening the edges using a brush and water, then pressing them together to make a square pot.

Building with bricks

This is suitable for children who are ready to learn to cut items to the same size. You may want to give it two or three sessions.

Knowledge resource: Have the children examine walls and draw the brick patterns. In the classroom, the children can build the walls using cardboard boxes. You could also have the children draw wall patterns using a computer. Make a pile of bricks on the screen (draw, copy, paste) and show the children how to drag bricks from the pile to build walls.

Focused activity: Give the children some clay, a board and a roller to make a clay slab about $1/2$ cm thick. Show them how to cut long strips $1/2$ cm wide from the clay using a ruler and a plastic knife. Have the children cut 'bricks' 2cm long from the strips of clay. Show them how to build a wall using the bricks.

Designing and making activity: Read a story, such as, *A New House for Eeyore* (adapted from the stories of A.A. Milne). Ask the children how they might build a house (with a single storey). Point out that a roof is not made of bricks. Ask how they will make a roof for the house. Have them draw a picture of the house they want to make and then build it.

Closing event: Return to the story you used for the context and have the children evaluate the house's suitability for Eeyore.

Using wood

Pig cabins

This is an opportunity for children to work with ready-cut wood (for instance, lollipop sticks) or wood that can be cut with safety snips (for example, thin, straight lengths of twig). It is better for older children in this stage. Allow at least one, long session.

Focused activity: Tell the children the tale of the *Three Little Pigs*. One house was built of straw, another of wood and a third of bricks. Following the guidance of the children, build a straw house (using art straws if real straw is not available). Have the children test the house for strength.

Designing and making task: Show the children some wood (for example, twigs or lollipop sticks). Compare wood and straw. Ask the children which will make a better house and ask for their reasons. Have them draw a picture of their house and use it to explain what they will do. Let them build and test their houses.

Closing event: Houses have windows. Ask what the pigs could do so that the wolf could not climb in through the windows. *Building with bricks* could be a next step.

See-saws

This introduces the see-saw action using a ready-made strip of wood and some card. It involves some manipulative skills and is better suited to older children in this stage. You may prefer to do these activities in one, longer session.

Knowledge resource: The nursery rhyme, *See-Saw, Margery Daw*, provides an introduction. Ask the children to describe a see-saw and how it works.

Focused activity: Show the children how to make see-saws from strips of wood about 30cm long and something to balance them on. Have them use play people or figures made from modelling clay to sit on the see-saw and make it work. Ask if a see-saw will still work if two people sit on one side and one sits on the other. Challenge them to get the see-saw to work.

Designing and making activity: Have the children use the strip of wood to make a pecking bird. Help them design and fit a beak and wings made from card. Ask how they can make it peck at the ground. (One way is shown in figure 5.14.)

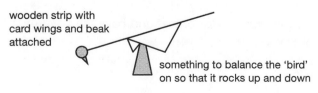

wooden strip with card wings and beak attached

something to balance the 'bird' on so that it rocks up and down

Figure 5.14 *A pecking bird.*

Closing event: Show a pair of scissors. Ask the children how a see-saw is like a pair of scissors (they are made from two 'see-saws').

Using wood in frameworks

The activities above do not involve much in the way of cutting and shaping wood but they help children appreciate some properties of the material. Some schools, however, like their children to develop these cutting and shaping skills early and use them to make frameworks. They commonly have children use square-section lengths of wood that can be cut easily with a junior hacksaw. For cutting, the children either hold the wood in a bench hook or use a small vice. They are given individual instruction

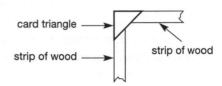

Figure 5.15 *Making a joint between two pieces of wood.*

first and are closely supervized at all times. Joints are usually strengthened by gluing small card triangles over them (following the approach pioneered by David Jinks, figure 5.15). The frames can be one, two, or three-dimensional (1D, 2D or 3D). Some suggestions for activities are listed below. How far you go depends on the capabilities of the children, the expectations of the school, and the time you give to D&T.

1D: A name card for the table

Early in the year, draw attention to the need to know who's who. The *focused activity* could be to have the children print their names using the computer then cut a length of wood and glue the name to the wood to stand on the table. The *designing and making activity* could be to make a name plate to hang on their bedroom door handle at home.

1D: A pedestrian crossing and bus stop

In Road Safety, have the children make a model street, including a pedestrian-crossing and bus-stop. The *focused activity* could be to make a lamp post to illuminate the crossing by cutting a length of wood, gluing a ping-pong ball to the top and holding the lamp post upright using modelling clay. A *designing and making activity* could be to have the children think of how they might make a bus-stop then make it.

1D: A shopping trolley

In a topic on Helping People, have the children think of something to help granny get the groceries home. The *focused activity* could be to make a shopping trolley from a paper handkerchief box using a length of dowel and cotton reels for wheels and a length of square section wood for the handle. A *designing and making activity* could be to make a wheely bin (using a tube) to collect small items of rubbish on each table.

2D: A picture frame

When the children have done some art work that you want to display, you could draw their attention to the way pictures are framed. As a *focused activity*, you then have the children make a frame from strip wood. A *designing and making activity* could be to make a window for a model house made from a box.

2D: A pencil tray

The children's pencils often roll off the table. Point out the need for something to stop that happening. Assuming that they made a picture frame, the *designing and making activity* would be to make a tray for the pencils. This could be a frame with a piece of card glued to the base.

3D: Beds for the Three Bears

One of the easiest ways for children to make three-dimensional frameworks is to have the children fix together 2D frames. For example, they could make a bed from three rectangular frames (figure 5.16). Houses can be made in the same way but, if they are large, they use a lot of wood.

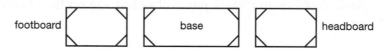

Figure 5.16 *Components of a bed.*

Using mixed materials and components

To some extent, many of the earlier tasks involve more than one material. The following tasks deliberately introduce more than one material to add to children's experience of combining them.

Tom and Jerry

This develops children's knowledge of a winding mechanism. It is better suited to older children in this stage. Allow an extended session to complete the sequence.

Focused activity: You could begin with a piece from a *Tom and Jerry* cartoon. After that, build a model of Tom chasing Jerry into a box (figure 5.17). Have the children predict and explain what will happen. When you turn the piece of dowel or pencil, the toy mouse 'runs' towards the hole in the box and Tom chases him.

Designing and making activity: Remind the children of *Little Miss Muffet*. Show them how to make a spider using pipe cleaners or woollen yarn. Ask how they would make it move as though it was real. If necessary, remind them of the *Tom and Jerry* idea. Ask them to make a spider that can come down onto Miss Muffet's head.

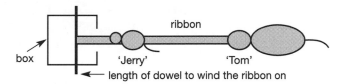

Figure 5.17 *Tom chases Jerry.*

Bendy things and snakes

These activities show children that rigid components can make flexible objects. Older children in this stage may benefit most from these. If you do all the activities, allow at least four sessions.

Knowledge resource: In science-related activities, have the children sort objects into those that are easy and those that are hard to bend.

Designing and making activity 1: Show the children a packet of 'worms' (popular bendy sweets). Ask what a worm should look like, feel like, and behave like. Ask if they can make a toy 'worm'. The children should try their ideas, aiming for a realistic worm.

Focused activity: Move from making 'worms' to making a bracelet. Begin by draping a worm around your wrist to link the last activity to this one. Does it make a good bracelet? What would a good bracelet be like? How might we make one? Show the children several ways of making flexible bracelets. You could, for instance:

● cut coloured plastic straws into 1cm lengths and thread the pieces on a shoe-lace;
● make holes in the soft plastic caps of juice cartons using a drawing pin then thread them on string using a bodkin;
● string together unwanted buttons.

Designing and making activity 2: There are a number of cheap bendy toys available, such as snakes. Show one to the children and have them explain how it works. Ask them to think of a way of making a bendy snake. You might set their thoughts in motion by showing them how to glue small boxes or blocks of wood onto a long ribbon (figure 5.18).

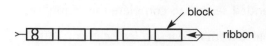

Figure 5.18 *A bendy snake.*

Closing event: Have the children seek out other objects that have been made flexible and explain them (for example, the coiled wire of a telephone, a chain).

CHAPTER 6

D&T Activities for 7 – 11 Year Olds

This chapter describes D&T activities for the 7 – 11 stage, also known as Key Stage 2 in several regions. Children develop in many ways in this stage: physically, emotionally, socially and in skills, such as reading and writing. At the same time, their knowledge resource grows considerably, partly through formal work in school and partly through informal experience in play and family life. It can be useful to think of this stage as comprising two sub-stages of children who are 7 – 9 years old and 9 – 11 years old. Although useful for planning, you must remember that there will be a spread of ability in your class. For instance, some 8 and 9 year old children may benefit from more demanding work while some 10 year olds may still benefit from the kind of work done by younger children. Equally, there will be children in one year group who are only a month older than children in the year below, so slight a difference that it cannot be ignored. At this level, teaching subject by subject is common. This does not mean that what is taught in D&T (or other subjects) is detached from what goes on in other areas of the curriculum. Where work in one area provides a useful context for work in another, it makes sense to take the opportunity and integrate learning. As with younger children, activities should be planned, organized and purposeful. Support the children to overcome what are insurmountable problems for them and, of course, some children will need more help than others.

With these older children, you will find yourself increasingly talking about various aspects of *Control* and *Structure*. Control is about getting things to do what you want. It can involve mechanisms such as, fasteners, hinges, pivots, push-pull rods, levers, return mechanisms, cams, gears, and pneumatic and hydraulic devices. It also includes electrical control with switches of various kinds and with electronic components like programmable switches. Structure has been described as why things do not fall down. It can involve working with particular shapes like, domes, tubes, corrugations and frames. It also includes shaping things to make them, for instance, lightweight, absorb shocks or behave like a spring.

The examples

Some examples of D&T-centred activities follow. The time needed for each one depends on the nature of the suggested activities. They often need several sessions of about an hour each to complete. Suggestions for how you might break up blocks of work are provided for guidance. You can digress, omit an activity or add others, according to the needs of the children. The *Contexts* are suggestions for giving the activities meaning and purpose. The *Knowledge resource* blocks refer to what you may need to develop for the activities. This may come from your teaching of another subject, such as Science. A *Focused activity* is a fairly structured activity to develop a particular D&T skill. When the children have the prerequisite skills or do not need to practise them, a focused activity may not be needed and the examples illustrate this. The focused activity is often too structured and closed to give a child sufficient opportunities for designing, problem-solving, being inventive and being creative. *Designing and making activities* are intended to do this. Suggestions for further learning activities are provided in the *Closing event*. *Some learning opportunities* are also listed. As in other stages, it is not a matter of giving the child an activity to do and letting them get on with it. It involves active teaching and involvement on your part if the children are to make the most of an activity.

After these examples is a stock of teaching ideas. These are taught in a similar way to those in the examples. At the beginning of this stage, you may have children who could still benefit from the activities listed for younger children. Use or adapt them to suit the needs of such children. Because this is a relatively long stage, the less demanding activities in each group are generally described earlier. This does not mean, however, that topics suggested for 7 – 9 year olds are not relevant to the needs of older children. If older children have not done a topic before, you can still use it (perhaps in a more mature context) but expect more of the problem-solving. You may also judge that some of the younger children in this stage are able to attempt some of the more 'difficult' problems. A Planning Sheet to help you develop such ideas, including ideas you have yourself, is provided at the end of the *Appendix*.

The problem with my garage

The task lends itself to a variety of solutions and is one where the children are likely to have enough know-how to attempt it without the need for a focused activity. It may be that the children devise something you know is feasible but beyond their present capabilities. If so, consider making it possible to pursue the idea. Both younger and older children in this stage could attempt this task although the solutions are likely to be different. Allow a session of at least an hour to complete the task.

Knowledge resource

Have the children sit upright in their seats. Ask what they can see. What can they not see? Tell them it is like that in your car. You cannot see the front bumper from the inside. This is a problem in your garage because sometimes you drive too far forward and touch the wall. Sooner or later, you will dent something.

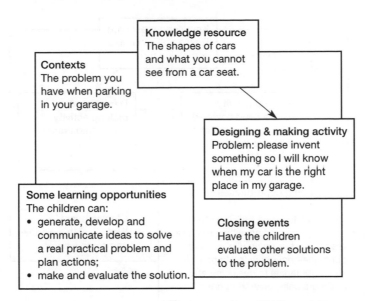

Figure 6.1 *Outline of an activity based on a 'real-world' practical problem.*

Designing and making activity

Have the children design and make something that will let you know when your car is in the right place. (Give the children a toy car or box to help them think and to test ideas.)

Closing event

Tell the children about other solutions (for example, a brick on the floor, a sponge hanging on a length of string from the roof which touches the windscreen when the car is in the right place, a switch on the floor that puts a light on when a car wheel goes over it). Have the children consider the strengths and weaknesses of these solutions.

Mechanical energy transfer: a powered fan and buggy

How to make a self-powered device is not something that is generally discovered by children unaided. This introduces some possibilities. It suits older children in this stage and needs three or four sessions.

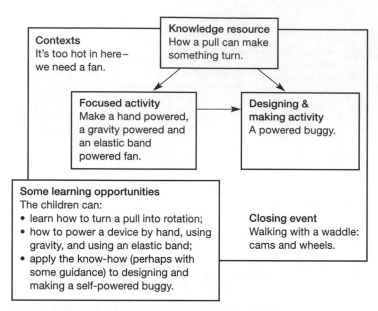

Figure 6.2 *Outline of a sequence of activities to develop and apply device knowledge to do with making things turn.*

Knowledge resource

To introduce some useful device knowledge, have two children hold a sweeping brush loosely, one at each end. Attach string to the middle of the handle with adhesive tape. To the other end of the string, attach a toy car. Have the children turn the brush so that the string winds onto the handle and pulls the car along the floor towards them. Next, make the car 'drive' away. As it pulls on the string, it makes the brush rotate. The children see that a pull can be made to turn something. Next, replace the car with a large elastic band. Wind up the string then stretch the elastic band and show that it pulls on the string and makes the brush turn.

Focused activities

On a warm day, fan yourself but complain that it is hard work. You need a fan that works by itself. Can they make one? Have the children make a hand-powered fan (figure 6.3a). After trying it out, ask the children if they can use a lump of clay to make it work (6.3b). Next, attach an elastic band to the end of the string. Put a length of dowel through it then wind up the string until the band is taut. When released, it should make the fan turn (6.3c).

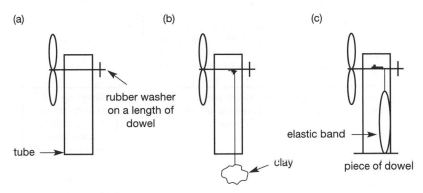

(a)   (b)   (c)

rubber washer
on a length of
dowel

tube

elastic band

clay

piece of dowel

Figure 6.3 *Making a powered fan.*

Designing and making activity

Have the children design and make an elastic band powered buggy. It could, for example, be made with a frame (see *Land yacht*), or from a box with two axles through it. One solution is to attach one end of the elastic band to the frame or box and wrap the other end around an axle, winding the axle to stretch the band. Some guidance may be needed.

Closing event

Have the children convert the buggy into a waddling animal. For example, the waddle can be produced by replacing the wheels with cams or by drilling off-centre axle holes in the wheels.

Food for a purpose

This is to illustrate a short sequence of activities on a topic suggested for older children. It reflects the children's increased ability to learn at greater depth and in a more sustained way. Allow two generous sessions for the food activities and more if you include others. Check for food allergies and respect food preferences and prohibitions (see also *Using food*, in the section describing *D&T activities in outline for the 7 – 11 stage*).

Knowledge resource

Food is often made in a way that does more than make it tasty and nutritious. For instance, biscuits are baked until they are dry. If they are kept dry, they will not go mouldy. In other words, biscuits can be kept for a long time. In the days of sailing ships, biscuits were a part of most meals for sailors. These biscuits were not the

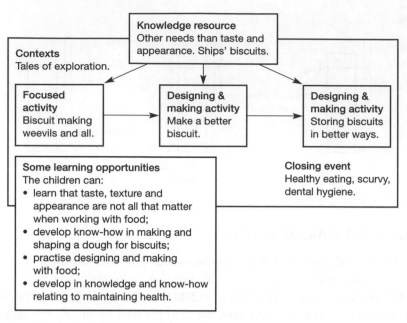

Figure 6.4 *Outline of activities based on working with food.*

sweet ones we know today but were made only from flour and water and were very hard. Even so, they became damp on long voyages and then became infested with weevils. Sailors had to eat them, whatever their state.

Focused activity

Choose a biscuit recipe that you think the children will like, is relatively easy to make, and suits the available ingredients. (If you prefer, you could buy a box of ready-mixed ingredients.) Show the children how to make the biscuit dough and add a sprinkling of long grained rice (as the weevils). Show the children how to roll the dough out thinly and use a biscuit cutter. Bake the biscuits for the children. While the children are waiting for the biscuits to bake, have them design and make a paper bag to put their biscuits in when they are cold. They should think about what to put on the packet to attract buyers.

Designing and making activity

Have the children consider whether real ships' biscuits (mainly made from flour and water) provide a good diet (ignoring the weevils). Could they make a better one? Provide a range of things the children might add to the biscuits instead of rice (for example, desiccated coconut, raisins, rolled oats, chopped glacé cherries, sesame seeds, dried apricots, dried bananas). Have them draw an evaluation chart and rate each item for taste and nutritional value. Have them design and make their biscuits, thinking about the best shape so that a lot could be stored in a small space.

Designing and making activity

While the biscuits are baking and cooling, ask the children how they might help their biscuits last longer. Discuss how they would keep them dry and free of weevils. Have them design and make a Longer Life for Biscuits packet.

Closing event

Show the children how to ice a biscuit and let them practise on a ginger snap. While the icing is still wet, show them how to sprinkle on hundreds and thousands, chocolate vermicelli, or decorate the biscuit with small sweets. This is also an opportunity to talk about dental hygiene and what too much sweet food can do to teeth unless they clean them thoroughly. Take the opportunity to tell the children how sailors developed scurvy on long voyages because of the lack of fresh citrus fruits and the vitamin C they contain. The sailors' teeth would drop out and they could die if untreated.

Using electricity: manual to electronic control of a road sign

In this, the children practise using electrical components and, if appropriate, using a programmable, electronic device. It is better suited to older children in this stage. Each step takes the child deeper into the problem. You could use as much or as little of the sequence as suits your needs. Allow about three sessions.

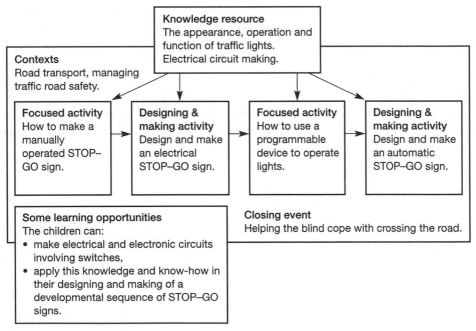

Figure 6.5 *Outline of a sequence of activities to do with a STOP–GO road sign.*

Knowledge resource

Remind the children of the appearance, operation and purpose of traffic lights, perhaps in conjunction with improving road safety behaviour. In science, work on simple circuits that include switches and light bulbs.

Focused activity

Provide the children with a kitchen roll tube and have them mark STOP and GO on red and green backgrounds on the side of the tube. Show them how to make a paper tube with a window in it that will slide over the kitchen roll tube. This window should reveal STOP or GO when slid up and down the tube (figure 6.6).

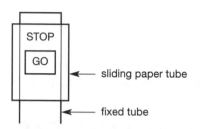

Figure 6.6 *A mechanical STOP–GO sign.*

Designing and making activity

Point out that this STOP–GO sign (figure 6.6) could be difficult to see at night. Have the children design and make an internally illuminated STOP–GO sign using bulbs, batteries, wires, switches and coloured sweet wrappers. For example, one design would be to dispose of the sliding tube, cut windows in the inner tube, cover them with green and red sweet wrappers and install light bulbs behind each window. Each bulb would be operated by its own switch.

Focused activity

Remind the children of programmable devices, like the battery-powered toys that some may have. Show them how to use an electronic unit that can switch devices on and off. Have them practise programming it.

Designing and making activity

Ask the children about the main drawback to their electrical STOP–GO sign (someone has to operate it). Challenge them to make an automatic STOP–GO sign using the electronic unit.

Closing event

Remind the children that some people do not see too well so they may not know when it is safe to cross the road. How can they help them? (One way is to have a buzzer in the circuit.)

D&T activities in outline for the 7 – 11 stage

Using paper and card

A pecking beach bird

Suggested for younger children in this stage, this involves using a stapler and card snips. Allow at least a session for each of the activities you include. They provide opportunities to acquire some device knowledge and apply it.

Knowledge resource: These activities could accompany work on the properties of elastic materials in science or on bird life.

Focused activity: Show the children a picture of birds on the shore looking for food. Have the children cut out a bird from a piece of rigid card. A 'worm', made from an elastic band, is stapled to the back of the bird's beak. The bird is fixed loosely to a block of wood using a drawing pin then the other end of the worm is pinned to the

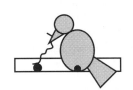

Figure 6.7 *A pecking bird.*

block similarly (figure 6.7). The bird strains at the worm when it is pulled back and returns to its original position for a rest. That is, the elastic band is a return mechanism.

Designing and making activity: Tell the children how such birds dig up shells to eat what is in them. The birds have to be quick because the shells snap shut when touched. Have the children design and make a shell that snaps shut. (At its simplest, it could be made from circles of thick card, hinged at the back and with an elastic band fitted.)

Closing event: Have the children look for other examples of return mechanisms (for example, door handles, catches).

Pushy Bugs Bunny

This involves the use of card snips and is suitable for younger children in this stage. The tasks include opportunities to acquire some device knowledge and apply it. At least one session for each activity will be needed.

Knowledge resource: Remind the children of work in science on forces (or do some).

Focused activity: Show the children a short *Bugs Bunny* cartoon. Show them how to cut out his head on a strip of card and insert it behind a guide so that it can be pushed into view then pulled down, out of sight (figure 6.8).

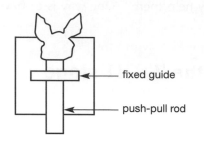

fixed guide

push-pull rod

Figure 6.8 *Bugs Bunny (rear view).*

Designing and making activity: Have the children design and make a *Bugs Bunny* Theatre (for example, a box like a TV with several figures that can pop up from behind a card). They should construct a short cartoon-style story to accompany it.

Closing event: Have the children look for other examples of push–pull rods around them (for example, a door bolt).

Talking heads

Suggested for younger children, this involves using card snips and paper fastener pivots. It is also an opportunity for children to acquire and use some device knowledge to do with levers.

Knowledge resource: These activities could accompany work on forces in science.

Focused activity: Show the children how to make an animal's head from card. Give it a hinged lower jaw using a paper fastener as a pivot. Have the children attach a lever to the lower jaw so that they can make it move.

Designing and making activity: Have the children design and make card cut outs of human heads with working jaws to make them look as though they are talking. Have the children use them as puppets to act out a simple story.

Closing event: Show the children a manufactured shadow-puppet. How is it like their puppet? How is it different? How does it work?

Bouncing biscuits

Suitable for all children in this stage, this needs safe scissors and introduces children to structures that will withstand shocks. It provides opportunities for solving a practical problem while taking the cost into account.

Design and making activity: Show the children a new pack of biscuits and complain that the end ones are always broken (having ensured that this is so beforehand). Open the packet, display the broken biscuits and suggest to the children that they should design and make a better packet. Allow them a range of priced materials to choose from (for example, 20p per sheet of A4 paper, 10p for 1 cm of adhesive tape, etc.) and a fixed budget (for example, 50p) and have them design and make a shock-absorbing packet for a biscuit. The packaging can be tested by dropping it on the floor. (The task can be made easier or harder by changing the kind of biscuit, by altering the budget, or by changing the height from which the packet is dropped.)

Closing event: Set up a packaging display (for example, egg boxes, tomato trays, shaped biscuit trays). Discuss the purpose of packaging and how the displayed items satisfy that purpose.

Memory pads

Suggested for younger children in this stage, this involves the use of a computer and printer to replicate patterns. Allow two sessions.

Knowledge resource: Have the children look for repeating patterns in their surroundings. In Art, you may have the children use a variety of hand-printing techniques to produce patterns.

Focused activity: Show the children how to make a simple motif on the computer screen (for example, by selecting from clip art or using the *draw* facility). Show them how to copy and paste to repeat the pattern to cover a page. You could let them practise by making wallpaper or brickwork for a model house (made from a card box).

Designing and making activity: Talk about how busy people sometimes forget to do things. Ask what they might do to help them remember. Show some small, decorated notelet pads and explain their use as *aide-mémoires*. Have the children design and make a sheet of small memo notelets, to be cut up and made into a pad by stapling them together along one edge.

Closing event: Set the children the task of finding something else that has been made like their memo notelets.

The galloping horse (or dinosaur, or dragon, or ...)

Suggested for older children in this stage, this involves the use of safety snips and the careful location of pivot points. Allow at least a session for each activity you include.

Knowledge resource: An investigation in science of how the position of the pivot affects the amount of movement of the ends of the lever can add significantly to the activities.

Focused activity: Show the children how to make a card animal with working legs. The model will need to be fairly large to give the children room to fit it together (figure 6.9). The circles are split-pin paper fasteners.

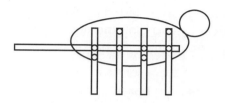

Figure 6.9 *A four-legged animal: when the tail is pushed and pulled the pairs of legs swing apart then together.*

Designing and making activity: Have the children design and make a human figure who looks as though he or she is walking. As this involves only two legs, it makes independent designing more manageable.

Closing event: Have the children explore their surroundings for examples of mechanisms like this. The simplest is a sneck-like door catch.

Shaped pads and cards

Suggested for older children in this stage, this involves the use of a saw or safety snips and a vice or clamp. It also provides experience of producing identical copies of a product.

Focused activity: Make a wad of paper (about 20 sheets) and add a piece of card at the back. Staple these together. Draw a simple outline of an animal on another piece of card and lie this on top of the wad. Hold the wad and card together with a vice or clamp. Show the children how to use a saw or safety snips to cut out the outline. Show how to tidy rough edges (for example, with snips or sandpaper). Remove the top card to reveal an animal-shaped notepad.

Designing and making activity: Have the children design and make a pack of ten identical postcards. They could, for instance, make cards in the outline of a local building or monument using ideas from leaflets from your local tourist office. The children could use the computer to produce the information for the card and print out a set for shaping.

Closing event: Have the children think of things that could be mass produced in this way. Point out that the parts of clothing, like shirts and blouses, are often cut out in this way. Ask: Why do it like that? See also *Designing and making* in the next topic.

Calendars and diaries

Suggested for older children in this stage, this involves the use of ICT. Allow about three or four sessions.

Knowledge resource: Help the children understand the nature and purpose of a calendar.

Focused activity: Remind the children that people welcome a new calendar at the beginning of a year. Ask how they might make one. Show the children how to use a computer to produce a month-by-month calendar (for example, under Windows, using a calendar template, or using a clip art package which includes calendar templates). Use a page for each month with a picture pasted on each page. Alternatively, have the children print out pages leaving space for their own pictures.

Designing and making activity: Check that the children know the difference between a diary and a calendar. Show some examples to clarify the difference. Challenge them to design and make a diary. You could have them use skills developed in *Shaped pads and cards*.

Closing event: Show the children a Filofax® and compare it with a diary. Have them examine how it is made.

Fold-away pictures

Suggested for older children in this stage, this involves making 3-D fold-away pictures from card and requires some forward thinking. Allow about two sessions.

Knowledge resource: Set the scene by having the children recall fold-away things designed to save space (for example, an ironing board, some chairs).

Focused activity: Show the children how to make a fold-away greetings card. Fold an A4 piece of card in half. On another piece of card, draw a circle and write in it, '10 Today!'. Cut out the circle leaving a foot to stand it on. Glue the foot to the inside of the card (figure 6.10). Cut a strip of card and glue one end to the back of the circle. With the card held open, judge the length of strip needed to hold the circle upright. Snip off the excess and glue the end to the card.

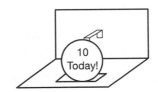

Figure 6.10 *A fold-away birthday card.*

Designing and making activity: Have the children design and make a picture book representing 'Four Seasons at Our School'. The book should have four fold-away pictures showing the school in different seasons of the year and text to explain it.

Closing event: Show the children a bought pop-up book. Compare it with what they have been doing.

Using fabrics and textiles

Lavender bags and fabric cases

Suggested for younger children in this stage, this involves sewing seams and concealing them. Allow about three sessions.

Knowledge resource: Display a pillowcase and turn it inside out to show the seam. Ask the children how the pillowcase was made and why the seam is concealed.

Focused activity: Have the children choose some loosely woven cloth and cut it out to size (for example, 20cm by 10cm). Show them how to thread a needle (with a needle threader, if necessary) and how to sew a simple running or overstitch to make a bag, leaving one side open. Then turn the bag inside out so that the seam is on the inside and stuff the bag with cotton wool. You add two or three drops of lavender oil. Show the children how to fold in the open side and stitch it. Have them design and make a gift tag for the lavender bag.

Designing and making activity: Have the children design and make a fabric case for one of their possessions, such as a comb or calculator. Emphasize the need for forethought as they will have to measure and cut a piece of material, allowing for seams. Have the children attend to the finish (for instance, if the case was of white cotton, it might be decorated with patterns or football team colours).

Closing event: Have the children examine clothes and shoes for seams. Compare them with what they have done.

A glove-puppet

Suggested for younger children in this stage, this task could follow the one above. It involves making and using a pattern. Allow about three sessions.

Knowledge resource: Show the children a simple glove-puppet. Turn it inside out and have them explain how it was made. Show them how to draw the outline of an animal on paper, allow for the seams then cut it out to use as a pattern. Demonstrate one way of using the pattern by lying it flat on some fabric and drawing around it. Ask how many matching pieces of fabric they will need.

Designing and making activity: Have the children design and make an animal glove-puppet. Emphasize the need to make the design simple and big enough for them to get a hand inside. Talk about how they can check the fit before they sew the parts together.

Closing event: Have the children examine a cloth glove and work out how it was made.

A string-puppet

Suggested for older children in this stage, the greatest demand is in adjusting the string lengths and in manipulating the easily-tangled parts. Allow two or more sessions, according to how you have the children make the puppet bodies.

Focused activity: Tell the children that the younger ones need some puppets to play with. Can they make some for them? Show the children how to make a simple puppet from a piece of cloth gathered into a ball with an elastic band and stuffed with scraps of fabric. Legs are made from thick string slipped under the elastic band. Suspend the body by a length of stout thread. Ask the children how they would make the legs move and how many threads they would need. Attach these and have children operate the legs. Point out that several people are needed to make it work. How can one person make it work? Show the children how to use strip wood to achieve this (figure 6.11).

Figure 6.11 *A string puppet.*

Designing and making activity: Have the children design and make people-puppets (that is, arms, legs, body and head).

Closing event: Puppets are often used in children's television programmes. Ask why it is hard to see the strings and how we might improve our puppets.

Sandals and mitts

Suggested for older children in this stage, this activity explores foot and hand 'garments' and involves making patterns. Allow about three sessions.

Knowledge resource: Ask the children when and why we wear sandals. Show them pictures of Greeks or Romans wearing sandals but point out that the Roman soldiers in Britain wore sandals, even in wet, cold weather. Their sandals had hobnails in them to make them last longer. Have the children examine a sandal and work out how it was made and what the straps do.

Focused activity: Have the children find out what is involved in making a pair of sandals. Give them a piece of stout card. They stand on the card, draw around their feet and cut out the shapes. These will be the soles. The children repeat this to make a set of 'inner' soles. They work out where the straps should go and choose a fabric for them. These are stapled from above to the upper surface of the soles, making sure that the ends of the staples cleat on the underside. The inner soles are now glued on top so make a card-strap-card sandwich. When dry, the children try them out and evaluate them.

Designing and making activity: In winter, it can be cold. How could they keep their hands warm? Give the children a range of fabrics to choose from and have them design and make warm mitts by tracing around their hands to make a pattern. Ask why they need to keep the thumbs separate.

Closing event: Examine other clothing that the Ancients used. For example, have the children experiment with a piece of cloth as a toga on top of their existing clothing. Is having to walk around with the loose ends over your arm a nuisance? What if you were a rich noble? What if you were a poor shoemaker? Did poor shoemakers wear togas?

Using food

Hygiene is an essential part of lessons to do with food. Remember also that some children may have a food allergy (for example, to nuts and certain fruits) so check with parents first and check the packages for reference to the presence or possibility of trace amounts of nuts. Respect food preferences and prohibitions; again check with parents first. As elsewhere, safety remains a concern. Also check use-by dates. Use only safe implements, show the children how to use tools safely and supervise them closely. You need to decide which parts of the tasks are best done by you. Heating, cooking and baking food are examples of processes you should do yourself, including switching appliances on and off and controlling the levels of heat.

Soups

Suggested for younger children in this stage, these tasks let children see that food can be a mix of several ingredients and the taste, texture and nutritional value depend on that mix. The soups need one session each and should be finished and disposed of in those sessions.

Knowledge resource: Have the children sort the contents of a packet of dried soup. Help them identify the constituents.

Focused activity: Show the children how to make a simple soup. For example, they might try a soup made from half a litre of water with a tablespoon of dried pearl barley, lentils, peas and long-grain rice added. (Soak the tablespoon of dried ingredients beforehand as per instructions on the packet. Add extra for the children to taste before making the soup.) Show the children how to peel and cut up a shallot under water and add it to the soup. Chop one half of a courgette into 1cm cubes. Have the children taste a small piece. Add to the mix and simmer for about 10 minutes. Divide the soup into two. Put some from one half into small cups for the children to taste. Show them mild red chilli powder. Add a little of the powder (up to half-a-teaspoon) to the other half of the soup and stir thoroughly. Have the children taste this version in their cups, as before.

Designing and making activity: Have the soaked ingredients ready, as above. Also have a variety of vegetables (for example, beans, carrots, cabbage, peas, potatoes). The children are to select ingredients and proportions and make their own soup.

Closing event: Talk about why we eat food and what we mean by a balanced diet. If the weather is warm, you could introduce cold soups – many recipe books include them.

Croutons

Suggested for younger children in this stage, this shows that bread can have a variety of forms. It could follow the above activity. Allow one session.

Knowledge resource: Show and talk about various forms of bread (for example, loaves, buns, bagels, toast). Have the children think of the amount of bread we eat. Ask what is eaten a lot in other countries (for instance, rice).

Focused activity: Show the children an alternative to bread on a plate with soup. Using scissors, cut the crust off a slice of bread and cut out some squares. Put them in a microwave oven on full for one minute. Let them cool on a baking tray then add them to soup as croutons.

Designing and making activity: Aunty is not feeling too good. The doctor has said she should eat more and soup would be good. Tempt her with some funny croutons on her soup. Have the children design and make them, then you microwave the shapes for the children.

Closing event: Show the children some bought croutons. Compare them with what they made.

Dips

Suggested for younger children in this stage, this gives them the opportunity to learn that there can be a wide variety of things in the food they eat. Allow one session.

Focused activity: Remind the children of an approaching event. Explain the concept of a dip used on such occasions. Give the children a small sample of a pickle (for example, a chutney or piccalilli). Have them use a fork to sort it and identify components. Have them check their findings against the list of ingredients on the container. Explain how pickles are made and that the vinegar preserves the ingredients. Have a range of breadsticks and pickles. Which bread and pickle combination do they like best? Why? Show the children how to make a dip from tomato ketchup or brown sauce and finely chopped items such as, shallot, tomato, cucumber, red cabbage.

Designing and making activity: Have the children think of other dips (for example, chocolate spread, jam, honey) and other things to dip (for instance, poppadams, crisps, mini Scotch pancakes, oatcakes, French toast). Have them devise and make a combination that they think will be good to eat. Ask how they would package and advertise it.

Closing event: Show the children some commercially-produced dips and examine the labels to see what is in them.

A celebration fruit cake

Suggested for older children in this stage, this involves making a cake but without using heat. Aim to complete the tasks in one session so that you do not have cakes in the classroom waiting to be finished.

Focused activity 1: To make eight small cakes, you need 200g of dried fruit mix, 50g of glacé ginger, grated rind of an orange, two teaspoons of orange juice (from the orange), and one teaspoon of mixed spice. Show the children how to chop the ingredients finely using a press-down food chopper on a chopping board (or use a blender and do it for the children). They add the orange juice and divide the mixture into eight. They then shape and press the mix by hand into cakes.

Focused activity 2: Show the children how to decorate one of the cakes. For example, you might spread on ready-made icing from a tube.

Designing and making activity: Have the children design a decoration for different occasions and try them on their cakes.

Closing event: Ask the children to find out how cakes are mass produced in bakeries.

Making eating easy: wraps

Suggested for older children in this stage, this introduces the concept of making things easier to eat. Allow two or three sessions, depending on what you include.

Knowledge resource: Talk about how food can be messy and can stain clothes. Ask how we manage food like this. For example, we put the messy bit between two slices of bread and call it a sandwich.

Focused activity: Show the children examples of 'wraps' for loose or messy food (for example, crêpes, tacos, chapattis, tortillas, fajitas). Have them practise wrapping ready-made crêpes into tubes around a filling. (Crêpes can be bought ready to fill and eat.)

Designing and making activity: Point out that crêpes can be soft and bendy if they simply roll them to make long tubes. Have the children design, make and package some filled crêpes (or other wrap) in a way that makes them keep their shape.

Closing event: Show the children a pitta-bread pocket. Ask how they might use it. Have them explore the possibilities. Talk about what is meant by convenience foods.

Using clay

Counters/Markers for a board game

Suggested for younger children in this stage. Any kind of clay may be used although you may find the clays that do not need firing to be more convenient. This activity involves rolling out the clay and pressing shapes from it. Allow at least a session for the activity.

Knowledge resource: Remind children of board games and how places are kept using counters. Show some examples to illustrate the variety of such games. Point out the need for rules.

Designing and making activity: Have the children generate ideas for a new board game then choose one and design it. This includes writing the rules and designing the counters. The latter are to be made from clay and finished in an attractive manner. The whole is to be packaged as for sale.

Closing event: Have the children try out their games and hence evaluate them.

Containers

Suggested for younger children in this stage, these activities involve using ready-made objects as moulds. Allow about four sessions to include time for the clay to harden and be finished.

Knowledge resource: Show the children some kitchen moulds (for example, for jelly or butter) and help them understand their purpose and how they are used.

Focused activity: Have the children roll some clay to form a pastry-like sheet. If necessary, place two lengths of wood on either side of the clay as rolling guides so that the clay does not become too thin. Show the children how to use a saucer as a mould. Cover the saucer with a piece of polythene or cling film. Place the clay on the covered saucer and mould it into shape. Use a damp sponge to smooth the surface of the moulded clay but avoid making the clay wet. Trim off surplus clay with a butter knife and leave to harden. The hardened clay may then be decorated.

Designing and making activity: Show the children some bulbs or seeds, according to the time of year and your other plans. Point out that you need something to grow them in. Have a variety of small, metal or plastic dishes they might use as moulds. Discuss why there needs to be a hole in the pot they will make. Have the children design and make a pot for bulbs (or seeds).

Closing event: The children could test their pots by planting something in them.

Tiles

Suggested for older children in this stage, this adds to the children's experience of working with clay and relates it to everyday uses in buildings and the home. It involves the rolling and cutting of clay. Allow two sessions and have tasks for the children to do while the clay dries.

Focused activity: When doing work on the Ancient World, show the children pictures of houses and draw attention to the roof tiles. Ask the children to explain why they are shaped as they are and how they work. Show the children how to roll out a lump of clay into an even thickness (place two lengths of thin strip wood on either side of the lump and roll the clay down to that level). Using a plastic knife, have them mark out the clay sheet carefully into equal-sized tiles then cut them out. Their first tile could be a plain, flat rectangle, like those common on many modern houses. After that they could try making the U-shaped tiles used on roofs in the Ancient World. Have the children make about three or four each of the same size. By pooling all the tiles made by one group, they should be able to lay them out in the overlapping pattern that channels water down the roof and prevents rain from entering.

Designing and making activity: Have the children reflect on what will happen to a table top if something hot is placed on it. If you have a trivet, show it and explain its purpose. What else could they use? Discuss ideas and encourage them to think about the properties of a clay tile. Have them design and make a pot-stand using clay. When hard, the clay should be made to look attractive so people want to use it.

Closing event: Ask the children to think of a way of preventing the tile scratching the table (for example, by gluing on felt pads as feet).

Using wood

Cleo the croc

Suggested for younger children in this stage, this involves sawing wood and develops children's knowledge of hinge use. Allow a session for each activity.

Focused activity: Tell the children about Peter Pan, Captain Hook and the crocodile. They then make a crocodile to accompany the story. Give each child a 30cm length of softwood, about 5cm wide and $\frac{1}{2}$cm thick (figure 6.12a). They cut about 10cm from this to make the upper jaw (figure 6.12b). The hinge is made from a piece of card slightly smaller than the upper jaw. This is glued into place as in (figure 6.12c). Use a thumb to make the jaw open and close.

Designing and making activity: There are crocodiles in the Nile and Egyptian children of 3000 years ago had toys like Cleo the Croc. Challenge the children to make another toy with a hinge like this (for example, a dog with a tail that can wag, a cat with eyes that can be opened). These need not be made entirely from wood.

Closing event: Hinges made like this but of leather were used until recent times, particularly on sheds and barns.

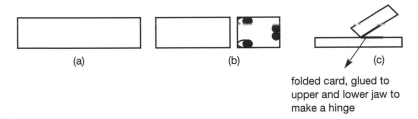

(a)   (b)   (c)

folded card, glued to
upper and lower jaw to
make a hinge

Figure 6.12 *Cleo the crocodile.*

Pencil-stand and street furniture

Suggested for younger children in this stage, this gives the children some experience of drilling holes in wood and fitting in lengths of dowel. Allow one session for the first task and two sessions for the second task.

Focused activity: Give the children a small block of softwood (for example, about 6cm square and 2cm thick). Show them how to drill a hole in it that is large enough for a pencil. Have the children make their own pencil-stand and finish it.

Designing and making activity: Talk about road safety. Set out a model street using boxes on a table. Have the children design and make warning road signs for the street. Ask them to think about how their pencil-stand idea might help them.

Closing event: Have the children look at classroom furniture for joints made by gluing one piece of wood into a hole made in another piece of wood.

Using square-section wood to make frameworks

Some schools have children make things with wooden frameworks from an early age and use the approach regularly (sometimes known as the frameworks or David Jinks approach, after its initiator). For instance, young children may make a chair for Teddy using lengths of wood with card triangles over the joints as stiffeners. They would use such frameworks regularly throughout school. The children could gain in two ways from the process. First, it gives them a way of making a wide range of products in the classroom. Second, it helps them understand the nature and purpose of frameworks outside the classroom, ranging from bridges and tower blocks to playground swings and clothes-horses. You are not, however, obliged to use this approach. Children can learn about frameworks in other ways. Depending on your school's approach to D&T, what you do may be in your hands but, given that the children should have some experience of working with wood and that strip wood is often easier to work with than other forms, it would be perverse not to take some advantage of the approach and incorporate it in your scheme (see also, *D&T activities in outline for the 5–7 stage, Using wood in frameworks* in Chapter 5).

2D: A land yacht

Suggested for younger children in this stage, some sawing of wood is involved. Allow at least two sessions.

Knowledge resource: Introduce children to frames in nature (for example, fences, skeletons, branches) and to manufactured frames (such as, scaffolding, tower cranes, pylons, tubular steel table and chair legs). Explain that they are strong but use less material, are lighter and often cheaper than solid structures.

Focused activity: Have the children make a land yacht. Each child saws a length of strip wood into four pieces that can be arranged into a rectangle. Have them cut right-angled triangles from thin card and glue them over the corners (figure 6.13a). They need eight triangles, four for each side of the rectangle. Have them cut four axle supports (bearings) from the card and punch holes in them (6.13b). Two of these are glued on each side of the frame (6.13c).

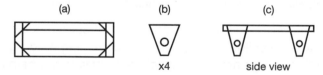

Figure 6.13 *Steps in making a land yacht framework.*

Choose dowel that fits the holes in the wheels. Have the children cut two matching axles from the dowel. They glue one wheel to each axle, fit the axles then glue on the other wheel to each axle (figure 6.14a). Note that children tend to make the axles excessively long and sometimes glue on all wheels before trying to fit the axles. Finally, the children cut a sail from card and glue it to one end of the frame (figure 6.14b). Blowing at the sail should make the yacht move freely.

Designing and making activity: Have the children consider how they might make the land yacht move, other than by blowing at it. Show them an inflated balloon and how it flies about when released. Ask if they can use a balloon. Have them design a solution and try it.

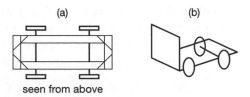

seen from above

Figure 6.14 *Assembling the yacht.*

Closing activity: The vehicle can be adapted in other ways. For example, strips of wood would make bench seats for passengers. Encourage the children to add extras to the basic frame.

2D: A tower crane

Suggested for younger children in this stage, these tasks build on basic framework making skills. Sawing of strip wood is involved. Allow at least two sessions.

Designing and making activity: Show the children a picture of a tower crane. Have them suggest how they might build one. To avoid building a three-dimensional frame at this stage, provide a box or kitchen roll tube for the tower. A long, thin, flat frame can be glue across this as the crane's arm. A bobbin will serve as a pulley at the end of the arm and a crank handle winder may be made from wire at the other end. A possible design is shown in figure 6.15.

Closing event: Explain what a conveyor belt does. The children can try fitting a second bobbin where the crank is and make the crane into a conveyor belt.

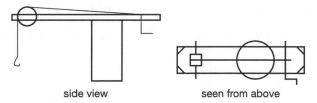

side view   seen from above

Figure 6.15 *A tower crane.*

3D: Space savers

Suggested for older children in this stage, these activities involve sawing and drilling wood to make a three-dimensional framework. Allow three or four sessions.

Knowledge resource: The designers of mobile homes have to make the most of the space that there is. Often, beds, tables and chairs have to fold-up or fold-away. Show the children pictures of mobile homes and their equipment.

Focused activity: Help the children design and make a folding stool using strip wood. Show them how to drill through the legs and insert a length of dowel like an axle.

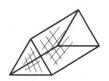

What will they sit on? Show them how to make a seat from a piece of fabric (figure 6.16).

Designing and making activity: Challenge the children to design and make a fold-up table or fold-away bed for a mobile home.

Figure 6.16 *A folding stool.*

Closing event: Have the children search a houseware catalogue to look for space savers. Have them explain how the space saving is achieved.

3D: Food covers and cloches

Suggested for older children in this stage, this practises the making of triangular shapes using strip wood. It requires a little more thought and care than the making of rectangles. Allow at least one session for each activity you have the children do.

Focused activity: Flies carry diseases. We must keep flies off food. One way is to use a food cover. Show the children how to make one using strip wood with card triangles to strengthen the joints. Help them choose an appropriate, open weave fabric

Figure 6.17 *A food cover.*

(figure 6.17). See if the children can understand that this triangular design is strong and saves on materials, cost and space.

Designing and making activity: Have the children sow some seeds in a pot and design and make a *cloche* to cover it (using transparent plastic from a bag instead of glass).

Closing event: Make a study of the use of triangles in bicycles, bridges and buildings.

3D: A Tudor house

Suggested for older children in this stage, this gives the children the opportunity to work on a more complex structure. Three-dimensional frameworks can consume your strip wood resources quickly. If this is a problem, make one model for the class-room. Allow three or four sessions.

Knowledge resource: This goes well with History work on topics such as, *Houses and Homes: Past and Present.*

Focused activity: Show the children a picture of a Tudor house and draw attention to the way its top floor overhangs the lower floor. This gave the owners bigger rooms without needing to own more land. Working collaboratively, help the children design and make a Tudor house for display in the classroom. Work with them to make a box-shaped framework for the bottom floor. Have them take turns to work on a bigger framework for the upper floor. The previous activity should help in designing and making a roof, otherwise, you will have to advise on making triangles. Have the children use card for floor and roof covers.

Designing and making activity: Have the children work in pairs or independently to produce furniture for the house using offcuts of strip wood to make three-dimensional frameworks.

Closing event: Using promotional materials produced by house builders, have the children compare Tudor and modern houses.

Using pneumatic components

Thing and friends

Suggested for younger children in this stage, these activities can be done with reclaimed materials, disposable plastic gloves and small plastic bags. Allow two sessions.

Knowledge resource: In science, you may wish to take the opportunity to focus on air and its physical properties.

Focused activity: In episodes of the *Addams Family*, Thing is a hand that has a life of its own. Have the children make one from a disposable plastic glove. Show them how to insert a plastic straw in the glove, gather the wrist around the straw and seal it with adhesive tape. Give the children small boxes (for example, tea bag boxes). They make a hole in the back and slide the straw through it so that the glove can be crushed gently into the box. Close the lid, making sure that it is loose. When the children blow through the straw, the glove inflates, opens the lid and appears as Thing. (N.B. Some disposable gloves are very thin and burst if the children blow too hard.)

Designing and making activity: Have the children design and make a Jack/Jill in the Box operated by pneumatics. Give them small plastic bags to inflate. Ask how they can make it look like a Jack or Jill (for example, by giving it a loose felt cover and eyes, nose and a mouth glued onto the felt). Ask what they will put it in (a plastic plant pot can work well if it has a hole in the base for the straw).

Closing event: Talk about other uses of pneumatics (for example, car airbags, inflatable cushions and beds, footballs).

Rory the Lion

Suggested for younger children in this stage, these activities can be done with reclaimed materials and balloons. Allow at least two sessions.

Knowledge resource: As for the above task.

Focused activity: Make *Rory the Lion* with the children's help. Use a large cardboard box for the body and a smaller box for the head. Cut the smaller box in half (figure 6.18). Hinge the halves at the back with adhesive tape. Insert a tube through the hinge and fit a balloon on the end inside the box. When the balloon is inflated, the box should open like a mouth. If the balloon is not big enough to lift the top, fill the bottom jaw with small boxes. Fix the head on the body. Have the children suggest ways of making the lion look more lion-like. Sterilize the tube using a baby's bottle sterilizing fluid and demonstrate the action.

Figure 6.18 *A balloon-operated lion.*

Designing and making activity: Have the children think of other things the balloon might do. For instance, it could make a giant clam shell open and close. Have them develop their ideas into designs and make them.

Closing event: Most bicycles have pneumatic tyres. Tell the children how tyres were once solid. Which is better, a solid or a pneumatic tyre?

Helping nurses help patients

Suggested for older children in this stage, this focuses the children's thinking on how to use pistons to make things move. It involves the use of disposable, plastic syringes (without needles). Allow about two sessions.

Knowledge resource: Unscrew a bicycle pump and show the piston. Discuss how it works. The pistons of such pumps are usually greasy. Ask why (to make the piston airtight). Show the children a syringe and compare it with the bicycle pump. (It may be appropriate to warn children never to touch syringes they may find in the street.) Connect together two syringes with a tube. Show that pressing the plunger of one syringe makes the other move. Have the children explain it. Connect together a large and a small syringe. Show that pressing the large syringe a small distance make the piston of the small syringe move a larger distance. Have the children explain this.

Focused activity: Remind the children that sick people may not be able to sit up in bed. In hospital, beds can be tilted to lift patients. Can we make a tilting bed? Discuss what is needed. Help the children design a tilting bed. For example, using a shoe box as the base, the lid of the box becomes the 'mattress'. Cut the lid across and stick it together again with adhesive tape so that the halves can be tilted. Place a syringe under one half of the 'mattress' and operate it with another syringe to make it tilt.

Designing and making activity: Nurses sometimes hurt their backs trying to help patients get out of bed. Have the children design and make something to help nurses lift patients off a bed.

Closing event: Draw the children's attention to other places where pistons can be seen. For example, those that lift the scoops on digging machines and on car boot lids. Note, however, that some pistons contain oil rather than air (because oil is not compressible – squashy – like air).

A rubbish crusher and car lift

Suggested for older children in this stage, this directs attention to the push of pistons. It involves the use of disposable, plastic syringes. Allow about three sessions.

Focused activity: Make a rubbish crusher with the children. Use a shoe box as a refuse lorry. Fit a piston in one end and fix a square of stout card to it (figure 6.19). Attach the syringe to a larger syringe by a tube so that the card can be pushed along the box to compress the rubbish (for instance, crumpled pieces of paper). Refuse lorries work a little like this.

Designing and making activity: Pistons can be used to lift cars. Have the children design and make a small crane that uses syringes to lift a toy car so it can be towed.

Closing event: Some things use pistons that are out of sight but we can hear the air used to make them work. Ask the children to recall the hiss when bus doors open and the hiss of a lorry operating its brakes.

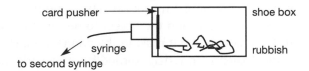

Figure 6.19 *A shoe box rubbish crusher.*

Using electrical components

Clocks

Suggested for older children in this stage, this uses a ready-made component (a clock) so that the children can design and make things that would not usually be feasible. The other materials are usually readily available. Allow at least two sessions.

Knowledge resource: Work on electricity prepares the way for this topic. In return, D&T activities using electricity can add to the understanding.

Focused activity: Battery-powered clocks can be very cheap. Remove the clock unit from its case, taking care with the press-on pointers. Discuss with the children what makes a good clock (for example, it needs to be high enough for all to see, it should be nice to look at and, of course, it should be reasonably accurate). Ask how they would make the clock unit into a classroom clock. Show the children how to fit the clock into a tall box (rather like a grandfather clock). Have them find or make pictures of the school. These are attached to the box in an attractive way.

Designing and making activity: Discuss how a bedside clock might be different to the classroom clock. Have the children design and make a bedside clock (for example, one design could be to fit the clock in a triangular box). Another would be to make a framework from strip wood, cover it with card and fit the clock into one face.

Closing event: Battery-powered clocks are common nowadays. Ask the children to tell you another way to power a clock (for example, using a spring). Ask what people used before there were clocks like this (for instance, sundials, water clocks, candle clocks, sand timers).

The Millennium Wheel

Suggested for older children in this stage, this activity uses a small, battery-powered electric motor. Fitting motors so that they do what you want is not always easy. Allow up to three sessions.

Knowledge resource: Work on electricity in science prepares the way for this topic. Have the children try out a battery-powered electric motor.

Designing and making activity: To make a motor do something useful, there needs to be a connection between the spindle and the object to be turned. This is often an elastic band. Talk with the children about making the connection. Have the children design and make a model Millennium Wheel, turned by an electric motor. One way of doing this is to glue a bobbin onto the spindle of the Wheel. The elastic band then goes around the bobbin and the spindle of the motor.

Closing event: Have the children describe toys which use electrical motors.

Special switches

Suggested for older children in this stage, this involves making a switch that operates a device when it is *not* pressed (that is, it is a NOT switch or NOT gate). The usual classroom equipment for learning about electricity is needed. Allow a session for the main activity.

Knowledge resource: Work on electricity in science prepares the way for this topic. In return, D&T activities using electricity can add to the understanding of the science.

Designing and making activity: Make a gold nugget by painting a hand-sized pebble or by wrapping it in foil. Tell the children that it is on display in a bank to attract people who might become customers. The problem is that Burglar Bill might snatch the nugget and run off with it. The bank needs an alarm that will go off when Bill lifts the nugget off the stand (that is, when the nugget is lifted, something should move and complete a circuit which sets a buzzer off). The children will need wires, a battery, a buzzer (or light bulb, if you prefer), cooking foil to make the parts that move, card to make springy bits, drawing pins and a board to pin things on.

Closing event: Draw attention to the light that comes on when the refrigerator door is *not* closed. Have the children think of other places where NOT switches like this would be useful.

A programmed switch

Suggested for older children in this stage, these activities involve designing and making a switch that does several things in a sequence. Components used in learning about electricity are needed. Allow at least one session.

Knowledge resource: Work on electricity in science prepares the way for this topic. In return, D&T activities using electricity can add to the understanding of the science.

Focused activity: Show the children how to make a switch that will switch a light on and off in a sequence. Pin a piece of cooking foil to a board. Cut a pattern of slots in a card. Pin the card over the cooking foil. Make the circuit (figure 6.20) and run the wire slowly across the slots in the direction of the arrow so that the bare end touches the foil in the gaps. The bulb will be on when it touches the foil and off when it does not. The slots shown in the diagram would make the bulb give two long flashes followed by three short flashes (going from left to right).

Designing and making activity: Have the children find out about the Morse Code and then design and make a programmed switch that makes an SOS call, either with light from a bulb or with sound from a buzzer. The more recent distress call is, of course, 'Mayday' (*M'aidez*).

Closing event: Have the children think of where programmed switches could be useful.

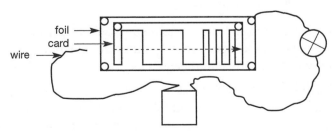

Figure 6.20 *A programmed switch.*

Using mixed materials and components

Few of the above activities involve only one material and children use components when working with kits and electricity. Nevertheless, this section sets out activities with the specific aim of bringing different materials together.

The problem with wheels

Suggested for younger children in this stage, this problem-solving task has children think laterally to make a buggy that moves but does not use ready-made wheels. Simple cutting tools, like safety snips, will be needed. Allow at least two sessions.

Designing and making activity: Have the children design and make a buggy. Tell the children that you have plenty of boxes for buggies but there are no wheels. What will they do? If necessary, show how books can be moved on rollers (like bobbins) and on balls (like ping-pong balls or marbles).

Closing event: Talk about moving heavy objects using rollers.

The problem with snow

Suggested for younger children in this stage, this activity is a seasonal one. This problem-solving task involves using a hammer and nails. Allow one session.

Designing and making activity: Point out the problem of snow in the playground. People may slip or get snow inside their shoes. Ask how snow is cleared from roads. How do people clear it from paths? What could we make to clear a path for them? Help the children arrive at simple solutions, such as making a snow pusher by attaching a sheet of corrugated plastic to a length of wood.

Closing event: Talk about snow ploughs and bulldozers.

Information leaflets (using ICT)

Suggested for younger children in this stage, this problem involves the use of a computer to produce a leaflet. Allow two sessions.

Knowledge resource: Show the children some guide books and leaflets and explain their purpose. Have them look for common features (for example, pictures, maps, instructions on how to get there, entry fees).

Designing and making activity: Tell the children that people often visit the school and that they need a leaflet they could use and take away with them. What should be in it? How can they collect the information? How will they build up the leaflet? How will they make copies?

Closing event: A forthcoming event needs a leaflet to let parents know about it. Have the children design and make one.

The problem with high-sided cars

Suggested for older children in this stage, this problem does not place great demands on tool use but requires thought in designing. It refines ideas about stability that may have been developed earlier. Allow a session.

Designing and making activity: Help the children grasp the problem. Show them pictures of low and high-sided cars to illustrate what you mean by the terms. Use boxes to show that high-sided vehicles cannot be tilted as far as low-sided vehicles without falling over. Show the children that tall candles fall over easily. Ask why. Candles that fall over are dangerous. How can we keep them upright? Which is the best candle holder to keep a candle upright? Give the children a high-sided box as the car. Have them make it look a little more like a car. Their challenge is to make it more stable (for example, they could make the base of the car wider or add weight low down in the car).

Closing event: Show a picture of a farm tractor. Point out that it is high-sided and is used in steep fields. They sometimes fall over. A cure is to attach a heavy block of concrete to the underside.

The problem with paper-work

Suggested for older children in this stage, this problem lends itself to a wide variety of solutions. Allow about two sessions.

Designing and making activity: Tell the children about the amount of paper-work you have. The problem with paper is that it is soon hidden under the ever-growing pile and you forget to do things. You really need something to organize your notes. Review possibilities (for example, a pin board, bulldog clips, labelled paper-weights). Have the children design and make a paper organizer for you. (For instance, they might make a rectangular board with bulldog clips attached along the top edge.)

Closing event: Discuss other 'problems' (such as, 'I can never find a paper clip when I want one.'). Have the children generate potential solutions.

Environments: Airport and Moonbase

Suggested for younger children in this stage, these activities use reclaimed materials and involve co-operative working. They could take at least two sessions for each one.

Knowledge resource: You may want to teach about flight (aeroplanes, birds and winged seeds), parachutes and rockets (Earth in Space) as a background for the problems. This is not essential.

Designing and making activity 1: This is the less demanding of the two problems as children are likely to have more background knowledge to draw on. The task is to design and make a model airport that takes care of all the passengers' needs (for instance, snacks, seats, toilets, check-in places, luggage processing, runways, aircraft, hangars). Have the children plan what they need to make in groups. Provide a large flat surface for the display.

Designing and making activity 2: Discuss with the children what it is like on the moon (for example, no air to breathe, nothing to eat). Working in pairs, have them design and make a Moon House. Arrange the houses to make *Moonbase Zeta*.

Closing event: Discuss what they would do if they went camping and forgot to take a tent.

Environments: Adventure playground

Suggested for younger children in this stage, this problem uses mainly reclaimed materials and could involve co-operative or independent working. Allow up to two sessions.

Knowledge resource: Visit an adventure playground or show children pictures of one. Have them explain how the activities work.

Designing and making activity: Have the children design and make a model of a new activity for the adventure playground.

Closing event: Assemble the models in an 'adventure playground' display. Involve the children in designing the display.

Environments: A railway

Suggested for older children in this stage, this problem involves working as a loose team with pairs of children contributing to the overall solution. The children have to think about scale. Allow three or four sessions.

Knowledge resource: Read *The Railway Children* by E. Nesbit to the children. Discuss the nature of a railway. What buildings and vehicles are involved? How do trains stay on the tracks?

Designing and making activity: The task is to make a railway system. Set out two long pieces of strip wood as railway lines. What is made will have to fit the lines or look right if placed next to it (not too big, not too small). Point this out to the children. Take ideas for what is needed (such as a station, platform, locomotive, carriages, trucks, signals). Have the children volunteer in pairs to design and make something for the railway.

Closing events: Arrange the models into a railway system. Trains need timetables. Have the children use ICT to produce a timetable for their railway, including excursions, advertisements and tickets.

CHAPTER 7

Talking about D&T

What has talk to do with D&T? Surely, D&T is about doing things, not talking about them? But talk can support thinking and, through that, understanding. Specifically, talk in D&T can:

- provide a context that gives tasks meaning and is motivating;

- support thoughtful working;

- develop D&T knowledge and know-how.

Providing a context

The first example is largely to do with providing a meaningful context for a practical problem. It does this through a traditional tale from India. To help the children think, you need a cardboard box with bars drawn on it to make it look like a cage for a tiger.

Sanjeev and the Tiger

Once upon a time, in India, there was a man called Sanjeev. One day, as he was walking through the forest, he came to a clearing where the sun beat down. Sanjeev jumped with fright. In the middle of the clearing was an enormous tiger, sitting in the bright sun. But when Sanjeev got over his fright, he saw he was quite safe because the tiger was trapped in a cage.

'Help!' mewed the tiger, pitifully.

Sanjeev approached the tiger slowly.

'Help!' said the tiger, again. 'Please, help. I've been sitting here in the hot sun for hours. There's nothing to drink and nothing to eat and I'm so hot I think I'll die.'

'Oh, dear!' said Sanjeev, feeling very sorry for the tiger. 'Oh, dear! But what can I do? I have no food or water.'

'Please let me out,' pleaded the tiger. 'Please, just lift one corner of the cage a little so I can slide out and look for something to eat and drink – if I'm still strong enough.'

'Oh, yes,' said Sanjeev, 'that's the least I can do,' and Sanjeev took a firm hold on the cage and was able to lift one corner just a little.

The enormous tiger lay flat on his belly, put his enormous paws through the gap, and pulled himself to freedom. Sanjeev held on until the tiger's tail was clear then let the cage crash to the ground.

'Rrrrroooooaaar!' went the tiger, rising to his full height and turning to Sanjeev, showing his big sharp teeth. 'Rrrrrrrooooooooooooooooaaaaaar!'

'Nnnnow then,' Sanjeev stuttered, 'Nnnnow thththen. Il've jjust sset you ffree. You wwouldn't hurt mme, wwould you?'

'Rrrrrrooooooaaar!' said the tiger, stepping closer and licking his lips. Sanjeev turned and fled. He grabbed an overhanging branch and leapt into a tree, climbing as fast and as high as he could.

The tiger ambled across to the tree and stared up at him. 'Oh dear,' said the tiger in a tired voice, 'why did you have to do that? It really is too hot for climbing trees. I'll just sit here until you come down.'

'You ungrateful beast,' shouted Sanjeev. 'Go away!' But the tiger sat down and began to lick his fur.

A little later, a fox strolled into the clearing. She saw the tiger and wisely kept her distance.

'What's going on?' she asked.

'Oh, nothing much,' said the tiger, 'I'm waiting for that man to come down so I can eat him.'

'Yes,' said Sanjeev, 'and after I helped him escape from that cage.'

The fox sat down and looked at the cage, at the tiger, and at the man in the tree.

'I don't believe it,' she said. 'No-one could be so silly as to set a tiger free like that.'

'Yes, it's true,' said the tiger. 'It really is.'

'No, no-one is as silly as that, even a man,' said the fox.

'Well he was!' said the tiger, a little annoyed. 'He really was, and I'm the one who tricked him. It's not just foxes who are clever you know.'

'Hmm!' said the fox, doubtfully.

'Look,' said the tiger, becoming really annoyed, 'it is true. Man, you tell him it's true.'

'Well...' said Sanjeev, not wanting to appear silly, even to a fox.

'Humph!' said the fox, scornfully. 'Tigers aren't that clever!'

'Now look,' said the tiger, standing to his full height and puffing out his chest, 'when I say it's true, it's true! I'm not having any fox tell me it's not true, because it is true. Just because I'm a tiger, you think people can trick me, don't you?'

'Well, someone caught you in the cage in the first place,' said the fox.

'Right! Just you watch. I'll show you. Man, come down here at once. We'll show this fox what really happened.'

With that, the tiger went back to the cage and Sanjeev slid down the tree.

'Lift one corner, like you did before,' ordered the tiger, so Sanjeev did.

The tiger flopped onto his belly, stretched out his paws and pulled himself through the gap into the cage. Sanjeev let the cage fall to the ground.

'Now then,' said the tiger, 'are you ready, fox?'

'Oh, yes. I'm ready,' replied the fox.

'C'mon, man, lift a corner and let me out again,' said the tiger.

Sanjeev looked at the fox and the fox looked at Sanjeev. Both smiled as they turned and walked away from the cage.

'Hey!' shouted the tiger. 'That's not what happened. Come back here! Let me out!' But the fox went home with Sanjeev and Sanjeev gave her a really good meal.

The problem is that, even though the tiger is dangerous, it would be cruel to leave it in the cage. How could Sanjeev let it out without being the tiger's dinner? Have the children draw and explain their ideas and, if feasible, try them out. You might conceal a happy, soft toy tiger under the box to amuse the children as they lift the box.

Supporting thoughtful working

Suppose you want the children to design and make a 'better' carrier bag (as, for instance, in *The problem with bags* in Chapter 5). You might set the scene with a bag that has burst, spilling its contents. The task is no longer abstract. The children see and grasp the need. They examine the bag and you ask them why it burst. This lets you judge their knowledge. If it is weak, you may have the children explore how paper bags tear, plastic bags stretch and handles give way. You use this to elicit ideas for making better bags. As the children design and make, you monitor them discreetly. You say to one child, 'I wonder why the bag is folded where the handle is.' You say to another, 'That seems strong. What makes it so strong? Why?'. To a third, you say, 'I see you are cutting your paper like that. Is there an easier way?'. When testing the bags, you press the children to think of how to overcome weaknesses and give reasons. Finally, you introduce a fabric bag and ask, 'How is it like the bags you made?' 'How is it different?' 'This one has four plastic feet. Is that a good idea?' 'Why?'.

This talk provided a meaningful context, something the children can think with. It helped them focus attention on what matters. It helped them organize thinking because connected thoughts are more durable than loose thoughts. It directed them to practise particular skills so that they make progress and their responses let you gauge understanding. This also gave the children practice in communicating ideas. You finished by introducing bags of a different kind and widening the context slightly.

Developing D&T knowledge and know-how

But not all D&T talk must provide contexts or support practical activity. Children can understand more than they can make. There are times when showing something, investigating why it looks like it does, how it works and what it does can be very worthwhile. For example, the pedal bin offers some valuable lessons. Lillian Gilbreth was a very busy woman – she had twelve children to look after and she wanted a bin with a lid. But most of the time, her hands were full. That left only her feet so she designed the pedal bin. When you push the pedal with your foot, it makes levers work to lift the lid – a hands-free pedal bin. Have the children examine a clean pedal bin and explain how it works. Ask them why people would want such a bin. Draw their attention to the foot-pedal, the lid and the material of the bin. It satisfies several needs: the operation is hands-free, it has a lid to keep flies out and smells in and it is made of a material that can be cleaned thoroughly and easily. In this case, they do not need to dismantle the bin physically but, on occasions, you may present artefacts that can literally be taken to pieces and re-assembled safely.

When would you use such a 'talkabout' task? Some tasks like this do not take long and can make good use of the spare few minutes you sometimes have near the end of sessions (not just D&T sessions). Others need longer to do them justice so you fit them into your schedule as a D&T session. However, do remember that these sessions are not substitutes for designing and making. They are intended to help children be more thoughtful about those processes and also help them learn what does not come so readily from the kind of practice they have in a primary classroom.

Examples of opportunities for D&T-related talk for the 3 – 5 stage

Products and case studies

Very young children are still exploring what to us are everyday objects. Take advantage of their interests by talking about how they work, focusing attention on 'special bits' that help us control them. This is a valuable contribution to their technological knowledge because they can usually understand more than they have the skill to make.

Jelly moulds

Show the children some jelly moulds and have them try to guess what they are. Show them how they are used.

Turning wheels

Show the children transparent toys with wheels and have them name the parts and explain how the wheels are able to turn.

Fasteners

Show various ways of fastening clothing (for example, a zip, button, hook and eye, Velcro® pad, shoe lace, press stud, and buckle). Have them try to explain how they work.

Pictures

Pictures allow you to bring other things into the classroom. You will have pictures that you use as stimulus materials to develop communication skills and some pictures will have a technological content. For example, pictures and some starting questions might be:

- children on a see-saw (How does it work? What would happen if two of you sat on this side?);

- Noddy in his car (How does he make the car go where he wants? What are these for? (pointing to the headlamps));

- the Bad Prince's castle (How does the drawbridge work? Why do they want to make it go up and down?).

Rhymes and stories

Some traditional rhymes have their origins in pre-industrial society and may not lend themselves readily to D&T talk. Nevertheless, some are useful. For instance, Jack and Jill's well has a crank handle winder with a rope and hook. To illustrate some possibilities, here is Humpty Dumpty.

Humpty Dumpty

> Humpty Dumpty sat on a wall,
>
> Humpty Dumpty had a great fall.
>
> All the king's horses and all the king's men,
>
> Couldn't put Humpty together again.

You could ask the children if Humpty Dumpty could have taken more care. What do people wear when they are on bicycles? What do people wear when they are on skateboards? Might a helmet, knee-pads and elbow-pads have helped Humpty Dumpty? Show a helmet and some pads and have the children explain how they help. What else could Humpty do? How do we carry eggs? Show an egg box and ask how it protects eggs. This gives the children experience of real world 'shock absorbers' in a meaningful context, an experience that you or others will draw on later.

Rosie Rabbit

This story provides a concrete context for a practical problem. The talk and real objects help the children grasp the problem and you encourage them to suggest ideas to solve it. You need a ruler (to serve as a plank) and a small box. Lean the ruler against the box so that one end is on the table and the other is in the air. Walk your fingers up the plank to represent Rosie.

> Rosie Rabbit lived in a field with a high hedge around it. She went to her favourite corner to sit in the sun but it was a mess! Freda the Farmer had dumped rubbish there! There was a box that Freda's new television had come in. And there was the plank she used to keep the barn door open. There they were, the plank leaning on the box with one end high in the air and the other end on the ground.
>
> 'I do wish people wouldn't mess up my field. After all, I don't put my rubbish in their houses,' said Rosie. 'I wonder what it's like in the next field.'

Rosie Rabbit had never seen the next field. The field where she lived had a high hedge all around it, much too high for Rosie. How could she see what the next field was like? Rosie had an idea. 'I'll use the plank,' she thought. 'I'll be able to see into the next field from the top.' Now remember that the plank was leaning on the box. Rosie stood on the bottom of the plank and up she went: front feet, back feet, front feet, back feet.

'Almost there,' she panted, just as the plank started to move. Slowly, it tipped down and now she was staring at the ground again. Rosie turned around and started up the plank again: front feet, back feet, front feet, back feet.

'Almost there,' she panted, and then the plank started to move again. Slowly, it tipped down and now she was staring at the ground once again.

'Oh dear!' said Rosie. 'I'll never see into the next field if it goes on like this.'

This describes the problem. Now you can pause and have the children explain what is happening. Ask how Rosie might solve the problem. Try the ideas and see if they work. This is what Rosie did.

Robert Rabbit came along and watched Rosie on the plank.

'Just the rabbit I want!' said Rosie. 'Come here, Robert. I've a job you'll be very good at.' Robert was suspicious. Rosie had played tricks on him before. Was this another one? He moved a little closer.

'Stand there,' said Rosie, 'on the end of the plank.'

'There?' asked Robert, but he stood on the plank all the same.

Rosie climbed on the plank in front of Robert and started up it again: front feet, back feet, front feet, back feet. Rosie got to the top and there was the other field. But she did not have time to look at it. Slowly, down went her end of the plank and up went Robert, high in the air.

'Oh, well!' said Rosie. 'This is my favourite field anyway,' and she stepped off the plank. Down came Robert with a thwack.

'Ow!' shouted Robert. 'You tricked me again!' he complained.

'Not really,' said Rosie, 'But look at the mess you've made with that plank and box. Don't you think you should take them away!'

Have the children model and explain Rosie's failed attempt at solving the problem. Ask how she might have made her idea work.

For more mature children in this stage, try *Sanjeev and the Tiger*, narrated above.

Examples of opportunities for D&T talk for the 5 – 7 stage

Products and case studies

Children continue to learn about their immediate world during this stage. The artefacts you use should reflect the children's increasing experience and ability to explain but, of course, not necessarily their ability to make them. For example:

Mechanical toys

Show the children a toy with a cam in it and have them explore and explain how it works.

Stuffed toys

Show the children an old, stuffed toy and disassemble it together, making a display of the pieces.

Safe kitchen devices

Show the children a safe, hand-powered food whisk and have them explain how it works.

Pencils

Pencils can have a variety of shapes: round, triangular and rectangular. Some are fat and some are thin. Have the children compare them. Which is best for writing their names? Why? Which might have been hardest to make? Why?

Shoe fasteners

There are various ways of fastening shoes: buckles on straps, Velcro® pads, laces, press studs, even zips. Have the children look at shoes and count how many of each kind there are. (They could stand in groups according to shoe fasteners.) Ask how they work. Are any of them hard to fasten? Which do they find the easiest to fasten?

Teapots

Teapots are notorious for their tendency to drip after pouring. Some are also awkward to handle. In a dish, give the children three different teapots, a plastic bottle of water and a plastic jug. Have them try out the teapots. Which is the best? Why? How could we use the drippy teapot so that it does not drip on the table?

Carrier bags

Provide the children with a range of carrier bags. Which do they think will be the strongest? What makes it strong?

Pictures

Pictures can remind children of artefacts, help them extend their vocabulary, and support them in explaining how things work. For example:

- a picture of a children's playground showing, for instance, a see-saw, a swing and a slide;

- a picture of a fairground showing, for instance, a merry-go-round, roller-coaster, and various stalls;

- a picture of a boating lake with rowing and paddle boats on it;

- a picture to accompany the story of the *Three Little Pigs* and their houses;

- a picture of a tricycle, pedal car or doll's pram or something similar with wheels;

- a picture of a Punch and Judy show;

- a picture of the street with street furniture and traffic.

Stories

Rhymes and stories can provide a motivating context for children. *Timothy Ted* is a story for young children about keeping cool and keeping warm. It can be used to help them think about the properties of various materials. To make the experience richer, have textiles, fabrics and garments that suit the story for the children to handle and comment on. Afterwards, you might set them the task of designing a hat to wear on a trip to the North Pole to see Santa or on a holiday to see Serge the Monkey in the jungle.

Timothy Ted Dresses Up

Timothy Ted is a Teddy bear with a pale brown, furry suit. Every night, he pulls down the zip and takes off his suit and goes to bed. And every day, he gets up, puts on his suit, zips it up and goes out to find his friends. But, on Monday, when he got out of bed. He looked out of the window and saw the sun shining warm and bright.

'What should I wear today?' he said. 'I've worn my brown furry suit every day for as long as I can remember. I feel like a change!'

He looked in his cupboard and found a big black coat. He put on a scarf, he put on some boots, he put on some gloves and looked at himself in the mirror.

'Just right!' he said, and he went out to find his friends.

'How scorching the sun is today,' he said, striding along the lane. 'How hot the breeze is today,' he said, walking along the lane. 'How warm the ground is,' he said, dragging his feet along the lane. 'Phew!' he panted, standing in the lane. 'I can't go any farther.' So he went home and stayed in until Tuesday.

When Timothy Ted got out of bed on Tuesday, he looked out of the window. The clouds were black and a chilly wind blew through the trees.

'What should I wear today?' he said. He put on a T-shirt, he put on some shorts, he put on some sandals and he looked at himself in the mirror.

'Just right!' he said, and he went out to find his friends.

'How cold those clouds make it today,' he said, creeping along the lane. 'How icy the breeze is today,' he said, striding along the lane. 'How frosty the ground feels today,' he said, running along the lane. 'Brrr!' he shivered, standing in the lane. 'I can't go any farther.' So he went home and stayed in until Wednesday.

When Timothy Ted got out of bed on Wednesday, he looked out of the window. The sun was out and the wind was blowing.

'What should I wear today?' he said, wanting to get it right. 'I know! I'll put on a bit of both.' So, he put on the shorts, he put on the hat, he put on the sandals, he put on the gloves and looked at himself in the mirror.

'Just right!' he said, and he went out to find his friends.

'How hot my hands are today,' he said, standing in the lane. 'How cold my legs are today,' he said, loafing in the lane. 'How hot my head is today,' he said, dawdling in the lane. 'How cold my feet are today,' he said, lolling in the lane. 'I don't feel right. I'm going home.' So he went home and stayed in until Thursday.

When Timothy Ted got out of bed on Thursday, he did not even look out of the window.

'Whatever I wear, it's always wrong,' he sighed. So he went to the cupboard, took out his fur suit and gave it a brush. 'I just look like any other Teddy,' he said, zipping it up and looking in the mirror. Then he went out to find his friends.

The sun shone bright and the wind blew hard.

'My head feels just right,' said Timothy Ted. 'My hands feel just right,' said Timothy Ted. 'My feet feel just right,' said Timothy Ted. 'In fact I feel right all over,' he said, skipping down the lane. 'Hey, look at me,' he shouted to his friends. 'I know why Teddy bears have a furry suit. I've got it right, at last.'

Examples of opportunities for D&T talk for the 7 – 11 stage

The transition from the 5 – 7 stage to the 7 – 11 stage is not a sharp one. Children continue to learn about their immediate world although this now encompasses more. With your help, they expand their horizons. The children's capabilities develop considerably during this stage so the examples cover a wide range in terms of demand.

Products and case studies

The bicycle

Have the children examine a bicycle, looking at its steering, seating, and means of propulsion. Name and explain the chain drive, the crank action pedals, and pneumatic tyres.

Hand tools, old and new

Have the children look for pictures of people using hand tools in ancient times and compare them with their modern equivalents (for example a mallet, saw, spade, pick). They have changed very little.

Helmet protection

Show the children a cycling helmet or hard hat. Ask how it does its job.

Old and new compared

Have the children compare an old device with its modern counterpart (such as a toaster, a kettle or a telephone).

Clothes hangers

There is a wide variety in the design of hangers for clothes. Collect about six and have the children compare and contrast them, working out what each would do the best.

Pegs

There are several different designs for pegs (as described in Chapter 1). Collect a variety of them and have the children sort them into groups and test and evaluate them. Have the children list what a good peg should do then use the list to evaluate each peg.

The safety pin

Fastening things temporarily can be a problem. A button is one solution but it has to be sewn into place. A pin will solve the problem, provided you do not prick yourself with it. And you cannot expect babies to know that some nappies may be held together with a pin that will come open if they kick their legs. This brief case study shows an invention as an improvement on what already existed.

> CASE STUDY Walter Hunt was an inventor in New York. He owed some money to another man but could not pay the debt. The other man gave him a piece of wire and challenged him to invent something new with it. If he did, he would be let off the debt. Walter bent and twisted the wire for three hours and, in the end, made a safe pin. When the pin was fastened, the point was safely hidden. What is more, the back of the pin was twisted into a springy coil so that, when fastened, the pin would not come open accidentally.

Show the children a large safety pin, like that for a nappy or kilt, and point out the springy coil and the hood to cover the point. Ask what makes it a 'safety' pin.

The pencil

Children are often curious about the origins of everyday things. This is an example.

> CASE STUDY The pencil is something we take for granted but it is a good example of the development of everyday things. The first 'pencils' were actually brushes made from tufts of fur bound to a stick and dipped in ink for writing. These date back to 1500 BC in Ancient Egypt. The Romans used a metal rod with a point on the end to write in the wax on wooden tablets. If they made a mistake, they rubbed out the marks with the back of the rod.
>
> Several materials have been used to write on paper. Lead is one of them so it has been used in pencils. Modern pencils contain graphite. To begin with, pieces of graphite were inserted into the ends of straws or twigs to make a pencil. But graphite was expensive and even the scraps were used by powdering it, mixing it with clay and moulding it into a long, thin rod. These clay/graphite rods were cased in wood to protect them. Nevertheless, they are still referred to as pencil leads even though they have no lead in them.

Provide the children with some straight twigs (the kind with some fairly soft pith in the centre). Give them some pencil leads and have them make a pencil by inserting the lead in the pith and gluing it in place. Ask them: Is a modern pencil better? How is it better?

The broom

This is another example of an everyday thing. The broom was, as its name suggests, originally a piece of the broom shrub. This could be used as it was to brush a floor but, with a handle fitted, the task becomes easier. Like this, the children would recognize it as the broom of witch stories. Something similar may be made from dry, tough grass. Show the children how such a plant can be used to sweep, even without a handle. The modern broom has clusters of bristles glued into holes in a block of wood but it still retained its plant name. You could have the children test a broom made from a handful of dry, tough grass.

A New Kind of Hut in Namibia

This case study takes the children beyond their local environment and introduces a problem in structures and the economics of building.
Some questions you might use to direct thought:

CASE STUDY It takes a lot of bricks and mortar to build a house so house-building is expensive. The Romans thought of a clever way to cut down on the cost. In those days, food and drink often came in big jars called amphoras. Just like we have lots of tin cans and bottles to get rid of, they had piles of amphoras. The Roman builders threw old amphoras into their concrete mix to make the concrete go further. Less concrete was needed and so the buildings were cheaper to build. Some of their buildings still stand today so the idea must have been a good one.

Two thousand years later, the Namibians are using the same idea. In northern Namibia, houses are built from wood but there is not enough of it. What they do have is a lot of empty bottles. Now, they begin to build a house by making a ring of mortar on the ground. On top of this, they lie bottles with their necks pointing out. Then they cover these with a layer of mortar and make another line of bottles on top with the necks pointing in. They go on like this until they have a circular wall higher than a person. Finally, they put on a thatched roof.

---

1. What is the problem the Romans were trying to solve?

2. Why does using giant vases (amphoras) help to solve the problem?

3. Why is the Namibian way of building a hut cheaper than using bricks and mortar?

4. Why are 'bottle' walls strong? (Think of a crash helmet.)

5. Does a house like this need windows to let light in?

6. How could you make a place for a door?

7. Suppose there was not enough wood for a door, what would you do instead?

8. Which house would last longer, one made of wood or one made of mortar and glass bottles? Why?

9. Can you think of a disadvantage of building like this? (For example, scorpions might live in the bottles; other people might look in through the bottles.)

The Statues of Easter Island

This case study describes the problem in moving large, heavy objects.

Case study In 1722, a Dutch sailor on his ship in the middle of the South Pacific found an island. As it was Easter Day, he called it Easter Island. To his surprise, there were enormous statues lined up, facing out to sea. They had giant heads on massive bodies and each one was carved from a single block of solid stone weighing several tonnes. But there were no roads, no horses, no wagons and no cranes. How had the people managed to put them there? No one knew because the statues had been put up long, long ago.

Use ICT to find a picture of the statues of Easter Island. Have the children discuss how the people might have moved them into position. Encourage them to use props (such as a block of wood for a statue and dowel for rollers) to support their explanation.

Pictures

Pictures that show situations for explanation and that suggest practical problems for exploration are very useful. For example:

● a picture showing a town or city scene and a variety of building materials and ways of building provides a starting point for talk about patterns in walls and roofs and their purpose;

● pictures of different kinds of bridges can be used to introduce talk about different ways of bridging a gap;

- a picture of a ship in full sail can be used to stimulate talk about what makes them move, how they change speed, how they raise sails, and how the ship is steered;

- pictures of early aeroplanes can introduce talk about how they turn left and right, and go up and down; it could also lead to talk about the history of flight;

- cut-away pictures that reveal the internal parts of objects can extend the children's drawing repertoire;

- show Heath-Robinson style pictures of fantastic combinations of mechanisms and have the children trace their action from beginning to end;

- pop-up picture books and greetings cards are, of course, objects of study themselves.

Stories

There are biographical stories of adventure and daring that suggest practical problems to solve. For instance, K. Davies' book, *Amelia Earhart Flies Around the World* might be used to provide a context for making a model airport (see *Environments: Airport and Moonbase*, Chapter 6). It might also suggest a need for compact packs of food and drink. Other stories might describe the products themselves as, for instance, in this account of the invention of cat's eyes road markers.

Percy's Cat's Eyes

One day, Percy Shaw was slowly driving home. It was so foggy he could hardly see where he was going. Even with the headlights on, he could barely see the side of the road. It was really scary because he knew that there was an enormous drop on one side. But he kept going, hoping for the best. Suddenly, he saw two small bright lights shining at him. He stamped on the brakes and did an emergency stop. Percy climbed out of the car and went to see what it was. To his surprise, a cat stared back at him out of the fog. The light from the headlights was bouncing off the cat's eyes straight back at him. Then Percy noticed what was behind the cat. Nothing! The cat's eyes had stopped him driving straight off the road and over the cliff.

After that, Percy thought a lot about seeing the cat's eyes in the fog. Could he make something like that himself? He stuck a pair of big glass marbles in a chunk of rubber and laid it on a road. The marbles behaved just like cat's eyes. Soon, mile after mile of road had Percy Shaw's marble eyes on them, marking out the lanes. Who can tell how many lives they have saved? It must be thousands. Nowadays, the cat's eyes on roads are even made in different colours to mark out different kinds of lanes.

To help the children grasp the idea and to start to talk about the invention, have them model a pair of cat's eyes using marbles or discs of cooking foil pressed into modelling clay.

Summary

Talk can prepare the children for an activity, it can support them during an activity, and it can pull things together and extend learning at any time. Children may use the same words as you and this can mislead you into thinking that they mean the same for them. But talk can reveal the difference in meaning and foster a growing understanding. 'Talkabouts' are products and solutions to practical problems that you show to the children for exploration and discussion. They give you an additional strategy for supporting learning in D&T and add variety to your teaching but they do not replace hands-on practical activity.

CHAPTER 8

Helping Children Make Progress in D&T

What is progress in D&T?

The word progress covers a variety of hand and mind matters. It can, for instance, mean learning a new skill, like using a pattern or template or sawing strip wood. It can also mean becoming better at such skills through practice. It may refer to acquiring new habits of thought and action, as when a child begins to work in a tidy and organized fashion. It may mean integrating learning as when a child successfully uses ICT skills to support and extend designing skills. It may relate to the development of interest and positive attitudes in D&T. These kinds of progress are important but the heart of the matter is helping children draw on their knowledge and know-how to become better practical problem-solvers, better inventors and better improvers. This means they should become better at, for instance:

- generating ideas;

- choosing an idea;

- developing the idea;

- communicating ideas (in various ways);

- planning a sequence of actions to bring the idea to fruition.

In doing this, they become more competent at, for instance:

- choosing materials;

- choosing tools;

- measuring and marking out;

- using tools;

- working to a plan;

- working thoughtfully;

- working safely;

- assembling, joining, combining;

- finishing products in ways that improve their function and/or appearance;

- recognizing strengths and weaknesses in products;

- recognizing strengths and weaknesses in the processes that gave rise to them;

- acting on these evaluations;

- applying their prior knowledge and skills;

- learning how to collect relevant information and develop new skills.

On the way, the children will develop a knowledge of some standard ways of doing things and learn the working properties of various materials. Given all there is to do, it is not surprising that some are neglected.

Some problems with helping children make progress

One danger is that progress in designing and making takes a back seat while acquiring new knowledge and skills does the driving. Tasks are chosen without considering what they might do for designing and making. Focused activities become the main event. Opportunities for creativity in problem-solving are reduced or disappear.

For example, when having children solve problems that call for a simple mechanism, there is the danger that we think of progress only in terms of which mechanism to teach next. While this is a legitimate concern, it is only a part of the progress we want the children to make. Suppose, for instance, your scheme of work indicates that you should teach the children about push–pull rods and levers this year. Focused activities may develop the children's knowledge and know-how but offer nothing to exercise problem-solving skills. Equally, you may set the children the problem of making a celebration card (that draws on their newly acquired push–pull rod know-how). Making another celebration card incorporating levers may not add much beyond some consolidation of skill and learning. There will be times when this is what you want but it should be the result of a conscious decision on your part.

A second problem is knowing what the processes mean at different ages. For example, children should try generating ideas but what does that mean for 5 year olds, 7 year olds and 11 year olds? Our expectations of children change as they grow older. This is reflected to some degree in the kinds of task we set. We tend to use very specific tasks with younger children but are less helpful and add more constraints as they get older. So, for instance, we might ask young children to design and make a tablecloth for the table that the Teddy Bears take for their picnic. With older children, this might be a problem in designing and making a cover for a patio table. Later, this could be designing and making disposable table 'linen' for use at a party and not exceeding a fixed budget for the materials. At the same time, we tend to move to less familiar contexts so that the children have to acquire knowledge to inform their designing. We also expect more skill and accuracy from older children and we believe that they should learn to deal with more complex problems and products. Older children will also have more knowledge to draw on and this opens up opportunities not available to younger children. In practice these increasing expectations relate to:

- a movement towards more open tasks;

- taking more constraints into account;

- working in less familiar contexts;

- more independent working;

- becoming more skilled and accurate;

- applying an increasing and more complex knowledge resource;

- working with more complex and longer tasks;

- working with skills, knowledge and know-how in more integrated ways.

Thinking about expectations like these can help you construct or choose a suitable activity. After that, you will have to think about what to do next. This problem is to do with the finer scale provision for progress.

Take generating ideas, for instance. The first step is to help children grasp the problem. You may do this with real objects. Take the problem, 'Teddy needs something to sit on so he can reach the table. Can we make something to help him?'. You show the children the Teddy and sit him on the 'floor' next to the 'table'. You point out that he is too low even to see what is on the plate. You ask where he would have to be to see the plate. 'Is that high enough to use his knife and fork?' 'How can he sit as high as that?'. You are likely to suggest a solution to a problem to begin with.

At a higher level of expectation, you might hint at the solution and lead them to it. Suppose the children have been set the task of thinking about how they stop their pencils falling off their table. To begin with, you may ask: 'Would it help if we stuck our pencils in a big lump of clay?' The next step could be to hint at a solution and guide the children to it.

Research shows that most 5 year olds can suggest an idea to solve a problem provided that they understand it. On this basis, you might raise your expectations further. To begin with, you may offer a few ideas that are clearly poor. For instance, when the children are thinking about how they might make a simple picture frame you might ask, 'Could we make one from pencils?'. You then ask the children to tell you why it is a bad idea. You follow that with: 'So, what would be a good idea?'

Moving to a yet higher level of expectation, the next step could be to press for alternatives. To begin with, it may be hard for children to reset their minds and think again so they are likely to need you to scaffold their thinking and progressively remove your support as they become more capable. For instance, you might ask how we could make a bracelet for mum. After some responses, you might spend some time exploring how many different bracelets they could make for mum.

In this sequence, the expectation arose from:

1. The child accepts your idea, to;

2. The child develops an idea from hints and under your guidance, to;

3. The child offers an idea with a few prompts from you, to;

4. The child offers an idea, to;

5. The child offers and considers several ideas.

Tasks and problems can also vary in their demand in other ways. For instance, the children may be able to suggest two or three bracelets they could make for mum but, if you followed that with, say, designing and making a creeping spider to accompany the story you are reading to them, they may have only one idea. Their knowledge of how to make things move may be limited to pulling things with strings so that is their one and only solution.

Experience teaches us which problems tend to have most meaning for children of a given age. In other words, you choose problems that suit the stage of development and experience of the children you teach and also offer the opportunities you know they need. For example, you may find that many in your class can generally offer an idea, develop its simple features, select materials from a limited range, communicate with the aid of their pictures, and plan two steps ahead. You may decide that it is time to set a problem where you can have the children focus on the 'special bit' in the design that the children tend to be vague about and have them make an additional picture which shows that part more clearly. In making, you have found that the children generally can choose and use tools adequately, mark out reasonably well and do things in the order they say they will but they do not work in a tidy, organized way. During this task, you decide you will provide cardboard box lids for the children to use as tool and material trays. You intend to press them to put tools and materials in these trays instead of spreading them out in a haphazard way on the table and floor. You have similarly found that the children can identify a strength and a weakness in their designing but rarely act on it when the next opportunity arises. You decide to target this by having the children recall what they said and take it into account when working.

Providing for the progress of individual children in D&T

Watching the children work and assessing their attainment will draw your attention to strengths, weaknesses and barriers to progress. How do you deal with these?

All children

Target weaknesses and barriers to progress. Choose or devise an activity that gives opportunities for progress in these. For instance, if the children are weak at preparing a plan of action you may have them design and make a picture frame. When they reach the point where planning is needed, describe the importance of forward planning, illustrate it with concrete examples, reminding them of those who glue both wheels on an axle and then try to fit it through the holes in the axle supports. Ask them what they will do first, second, and so on. Then use this to compile a list of actions. As they make the frame, you have them tick off each item in turn. If the list breaks down at some point, have the child revise it.

Many tasks offer opportunities for planning but not all are equally good for other things. For instance, some of the children may be weak at getting started. They tend to sit staring around without ideas. You may feel that they would benefit from some success so you work with the group before they begin the scheduled D&T activity. You could pose a problem, such as: 'You go out on a sunny day but, when you are too far away to dash home, it suddenly pours down. Your shoes are not waterproof. You know that your feet will soon be soaked and then you'll have to squelch around for the rest of the day in wet socks. How could you keep your feet dry in the downpour? Think of as many ways as you can.' You may have to start the ball rolling:

'You could take your shoes and socks off and put them under your T-shirt.'

'You could look for old plastic bags and put your feet inside them.'

'You could squat down with your feet under you and hold the bag up like an umbrella.'

You then take responses until they dry up so you prompt the children to think of what might be available around them and suggest more responses. Accept responses and make thinking of ideas fun. Now move on to the scheduled D&T activity and repeat the process.

On another occasion, you notice that one child's ideas tend to be very vague. His explanations are full of 'something that will ...'. Even handling and arranging the materials does not seem to make the ideas more concrete. You sit with this child and help him identify the 'something that will ...' bits. You focus his attention on them in turn and have him handle the materials to help him think about how he might overcome each mini-problem.

This helps you target weaknesses in a systematic way but remember that one intervention is unlikely to be enough. Keep intervening until new habits develop. You also have to think beyond weaknesses and move children forward with more demanding tasks and new experiences. To begin with, these may need your support just like the tasks above.

Lower attainers

Some children may be weak in several aspects of D&T but can be supported by approaches like those above. The weaknesses of others may be more general. You may need additional strategies to help them. Lower attainers often benefit from structure. Help them cope with a task by breaking it into stages. Provide worksheets with subtitles that guide thinking. As habits develop, progressively remove the scaffold.

Practical problems can often be solved at various levels. In other words, children solve a problem with the knowledge and know-how they have. Some solutions may be low-tech and others high-tech so one task may fit all. This is useful because it means you do not have to mark off certain children as 'different' by giving them different tasks. Nevertheless, if the children think you expect low attainers to produce the soon-to-fall-to-pieces, poorly finished product, then they will. One strategy you might use to help them make progress has seven steps:

1. Check for yourself that the child has the underlying skills.

2. Take the child's most recent design that was not successful. Help the child identify the main cause.

3. Introduce a more promising approach and discuss it.

4. Model the approach, using the most recent design to make it concrete.

5. Have the child rehearse what was done to establish it in the child's memory.

6. Set a task for the child to practise on. Choose one that lends itself to the approach.

7. Have the child use the approach in the next task.

This strategy needs your time and will probably have to be repeated to overcome the difficulty. Success does not always come easily or quickly.

Sometimes, you can tune the level of difficulty of a task to suit children's capabilities. For example, if you set the children the challenge of making a packet to protect a biscuit, it could have various levels of difficulty, such as:

●   Design and make a package to protect a ginger snap given an A2 sheet of newsprint paper, an A4 sheet of wrapping paper, and 30cm of adhesive tape. The package is to be tested by dropping it onto the carpet from a height of 1m.

●   Design and make a package to protect a digestive biscuit given an A3 sheet of newsprint paper, an A4 sheet of wrapping paper, and 15cm of adhesive tape. The package is to be tested by dropping it onto the carpet from a height of 2m.

●   Design and make a package to protect a digestive biscuit given two A4 sheets of wrapping paper, and 10cm of adhesive tape. The package is to be tested by dropping it down the stairwell.

- Design and make a package to protect a digestive biscuit given a budget of 45p. A4 paper costs 20p per sheet and adhesive tape costs 1p per cm. You can trade materials you do not need for something you do need with others. The package is to be tested by dropping it onto the carpet from a height of 2m.

You choose a level that will challenge the children but not one that is entirely beyond them.

Finally, you may set a task in a more specific way for some children. For example, take the problem: 'Can you make an animal that bites people for those in Mr X's class to play with?' It could be expressed as, 'Can you make a crocodile with jaws that bite ...' and, 'Can you make a crocodile like a giant pair of scissors so that its jaws bite ...' Often, the more specific the information, the easier the task.

Higher attainers

High attainers are those who are strong in most aspects of D&T. What has already been said also applies to helping these children make progress. Your role is to encourage these children to design and make in ways that produce more effective, more reliable and more pleasing solutions to the problems. A practical problem can often be solved in a variety of ways and these children need to solve them using higher levels of capability.

It is important that there is some worthwhile challenge in tasks for these children so that they do not mark time. For example, suppose the children had to design and make something for a model fairground. You can increase the level of demand of a given task by drawing on new knowledge, working with different materials, or by adding constraints. If such a child chooses to design and make a merry-go-round, you could require it to be battery-powered with flashing lights controlled by a black box of electronics. You might also expect the child to evaluate the product against criteria they have developed themselves at the design stage. As an extension, you may have the child learn how electricity was generated in fairgrounds using steam engines.

On occasions, you may decide that a different task would provide more challenge and extend such children's D&T capabilities in different ways. For instance, you may point out how there tends to be a crush in the dining hall, with children not observing the queuing rule so that younger children are pushed aside. Can they solve the problem? In the process, you expect them to observe the event, interview kitchen staff and teachers and collect information to help them identify the main causes. They then set about designing a system to solve the problem and prepare a report to submit to the head teacher.

Other matters

For some children, access is a problem. For example, children who are not fluent in English may not have grasped what you want them to do. Some strategies that may help are:

- using pictures, picture dictionaries and videotapes – but note that pictures do not always communicate actions or problems well;

- working alongside the child initially, modelling actions to make the child's task clear;

- asking for help from someone who speaks the child's language;

- peer tutoring by a child who is bilingual;

- using a computer programme that will translate from English into the child's language (and vice-versa).

Take opportunities to develop children's D&T English, helping them learn the names of tools, materials and phrases relating to safety.

Some children may have physical handicaps that limit access. For instance, a wheelchair may be essential for mobility but may be at the wrong height for using tools. It may also make it difficult to move close to a table. You may improve access by:

- ensuring that work areas are open and uncluttered;

- adjusting the height of a table;

- raising the height of the child by using boards to stand on;

- ensuring that tools are within easy reach or in trays;

- providing tools that can be used safely with one hand;

- providing quick-grip clamps to hold items firmly on a table surface;

- setting out materials so that they are easier to grasp;

- providing a clear path to the computer and printer.

And, of course, treat this provision as a matter of routine.

If a child is allergic to a material, use another material. When teaching partially-sighted children, set out tools in a safe and consistent way. Also use materials that can be distinguished by feel. Encourage children to develop their own way of working safely but make safety the first consideration. Those who are hard of hearing may not hear your warning or the noise of falling objects. They should work where they can see you and you should be close enough to intervene with any child.

Lists of what you might press the children to achieve

The lists below offer some progressive sequences that may help you plan for progress. They are to help you think about the fine detail of progress but these lists are only for guidance and are not definitive.

When thinking about progress, you may prefer to think of designing and making in terms of getting started, developing ideas, turning ideas into reality, and end matters. This is useful but remember that these stages do not have sharp boundaries (see also Chapter 2). You are likely to find some things in the lists below happening in more than one stage.

Designing

Grasping the problem

The child: relies on your interpretation of a specific problem; contributes to your interpretation of a specific problem; interprets a specific problem; relies on your interpretation of a more general problem; contributes to your interpretation of a more general problem; interprets a more general problem.

Generating ideas

The child: accepts your idea; develops an idea from hints and under your guidance; offers an idea with a few prompts from you; offers an idea; generates several feasible ideas; generates feasible ideas shaped by collected information; generates feasible ideas shaped by information from several sources.

Choosing an idea

The child: accepts the given idea; accepts his or her own idea; chooses an idea from two or more ideas; chooses an idea and has a rational reason for the choice; argues the pros and cons for the choice.

Developing an idea

The child: follows your instructions; makes tentative suggestions following hints for development from you; describes simple features of the proposal; describes simple features of the proposal and is aware of unresolved problems; attempts to address unresolved problems without prompting.

Materials

The child: uses the materials given; selects appropriate materials from a range of two or three different materials; selects appropriate materials from a range and justifies the choice on the grounds that it satisfies the task requirements; selects two materials to combine to produce a required practical property.

Communicating ideas

The child: describes an idea orally; describes an idea in a few sentences in writing; describes an idea at length in an orderly sequence: uses hands to help explain; uses a given model to help explain; improvises a simple model to help explain: uses an existing picture to support communication; draws a simple picture to help describe an idea; draws and uses different views to help describe an idea; draws and uses an exploded diagram to help explain.

Planning for action

The child: tells you what he or she will do next; tells you what he or she will do next and then after that; constructs a list describing (in pictures or words) the sequence of actions to be taken; divides a task into two sub-tasks and devises lists for both sub-tasks; constructs a list describing the sequence of actions to be taken showing awareness that there may be options or uncertainties at particular points.

Making

Choosing tools

The child: uses the given tool; finds and uses an identified tool amongst others; chooses an appropriate tool from three or four others; chooses an appropriate tool from a tool box.

Using tools and working safely

The child: uses the hands as tools (for example, in tearing and folding); avoids direct contact with points and edges; avoids direct contact with points and edges and describes the nature of the danger; holds a tool correctly; uses a tool correctly under your direct supervision showing a concern for the safety of self and others; uses a tool correctly under your general supervision showing a concern for the safety of self and others; works in a tidy, organized, safe way; uses tools correctly and safely and works in a tidy, organized, safe way as a habit.

Measuring and marking out

The child: recognizes when something will be too big or too small and adjusts it accordingly; gauges the required size by direct comparison and marks it on the material while in position; measures the required size with non-standard measures (for example, in cubes or pencil lengths) and transfers that to the material; measures the required size with a ruler and uses that to mark the length on the material; measures and marks out sizes so that the lines guide the shaping (for example, to guide a saw cut).

Working to plan and working thoughtfully

The child: follows your step-by-step instructions; does what was said will be done next; uses a plan of action; recognizes when a plan of action is failing; modifies a plan of action in use; works systematically to a branching plan; thinks ahead and anticipates potential problems.

Assembling, joining, combining

The child: puts the items together loosely before joining them; puts the items together loosely and makes adjustments before joining them; joins/combines materials permanently in simple ways (for example, by using a safe glue, stapling, or kneading) and loosely or temporarily in simple ways (for instance, by using a paper fastener or paper clip); joins/combines materials permanently in other ways (for example, by using a nail) and temporarily (for instance, by using a bolt or button).

Finishing

The child: applies an attractive finish using coloured pencils and water-based paints, applies additional coats to improve the finish; applies additional materials using a safe glue (for example, glitter, sand, felt, coloured papers) to make the product more pleasing; applies a finish that gives a gloss effect (for example, by applying a final coat of PVA adhesive on dry paint); devises effective fixing and decorative effects.

Evaluating

Identifying strengths and weaknesses in products

The child: tries out what they make; tries a product and generally comments on how well it works; tries a product, generally comments on how well it works and on what could be better; tries a product using a short tick list provided by you to evaluate it; identifies specific aspects of a product that work well and any that could be better and states what would make them better; constructs and uses a list of criteria for gauging the success of a product.

Identifying strengths and weaknesses in processes

The child: describes the making process; reflects on the making process and says what was easy and hard to do; reflects on the making process and tells you something that would be done in a different way next time; points to a difference between the design and the finished product (if any) and gives a reason for it; points to differences between the design and the finished product (if any) and tells you how the designing would be different if it was done again.

Acting on evaluations

The child: tries a different way of working in designing and/or making; recalls strengths and weaknesses and agrees a different way of working with you; recalls strengths and weaknesses and tries working in a different way, subject to your approval.

Summary

Progress involves change. In D&T, the change is in for instance, acquiring and developing skills and know-how, acquiring and developing habits of thought and action, and managing thought and action to solve practical problems. Care is needed to ensure that a wide range of hand and mind activities is provided. Do not leave progress to chance. Target existing weaknesses in learning and gently push the children to new experiences. Make sure that all children are being mentally stretched and ensure that all have access to the opportunities you provide.

CHAPTER 9

Assessing D&T

Assessment in D&T

Assessment in D&T judges how well children generate and handle ideas, plan and turn ideas into reality and evaluate them. Knowledge (as of elasticity, levers, the strength of certain structures and electrical circuits) is a resource children must draw on but, while we would look for a readiness to draw on it and use it flexibly, we tend not to assess it directly in D&T.

Why assess D&T?

Assessment in D&T can help you:

● gauge the effectiveness of your teaching and plan future activities;

● give feedback to children to shape their learning and tailor teaching to particular needs;

● inform others of the state of the children's learning;

● contribute data to a description of the learning in your school.

A problem with assessing D&T

Assessment in D&T is not a straightforward matter because it involves judging the quality of the D&T process. Suppose, for instance, you tell the children about the garage problem. Your car only just fits and sometimes you bump the wall in front of you. Sooner or later, you will damage your car. Can they solve the problem for you? Suppose a child brings you her solution. It comprises a battery-operated buzzer that is switched on by the front wheel of the car. You are very impressed by what you see but what you see is only a part of what is to be assessed. The child had to generate possible solutions, develop one, apply her knowledge of electrical circuits and components and test the idea, adjust the design, if necessary, plan a course of action and make, finish and test the device. During this time, she rejected a possible design, back-tracked and developed another. Even when making the device, it had to be adjusted to accommodate the battery and the connecting clips. The point is that you have the product but, behind it, are the thoughts and actions that gave rise to it. Often, you will also have the child's account of the design but adding this still does not give you the full story. For instance, how the child overcame the unexpected without your help will probably not be documented. Nor will there be a record of the way she learned to use clips to attach the wires to the base board. A significant part of the real and often messy process of designing and making is in the child's thoughts and actions. Such processes are only partly evident in the products (written accounts, pictures of designs, plans in the form of flow charts and final artefacts). We have to watch how the child works and ask questions that encourage her to reveal her thinking in order to build up a fuller picture of her capability. It is not simply a case of finding out that a child can draw and label a diagram, subdivide a task or collect and use information from potential users. Being able to do these things is important but we must also ask if a child can adapt them to suit the occasion and whether the child shows an increasing flexibility and independence in the process.

Assessing for good teaching

An ongoing concern will be for the children's progress. This involves knowing the effect of your teaching and using it to shape your future teaching. It is also about identifying the children's strengths and weaknesses in order to guide and advise them. Here are two examples, one on assessing younger children and the other on assessing older children.

Suppose you are teaching younger children and begin by reminding them of the story of *Goldilocks and the Three Bears*. You believe that the activity will provide a context for the children to acquire a new skill. It also gives them a chance to draw on existing knowledge for an idea, to explain it, to use the new skill to realize the idea, and to evaluate it.

Almost as props for the story, you have the children make a table from a shoe box. The problem is that Teddy cannot reach the table. He needs a cushion to sit on so he can see his bowl of porridge. You show the children how to staple along three sides of a folded rectangle of felt and pack it with scraps of fabric, closing the fourth side with staples. They try it for themselves. With Teddy sitting on the cushion, he can now see into what should have been his bowl of porridge. But, of course, Goldilocks ate it. Later, she tried out the beds. You show the children how to use the shoe box as a bed. The problem is that it is a rather hard bed and Teddy would not get much sleep on that. What does it need? How can they make blankets and a pillow for Teddy? The children draw pictures of what they will make and then make them. The products of these young children might include: ideas presented orally, Teddy's table, tablecloth and cushion, Teddy's bed, blankets and pillow, and an oral evaluation of the blankets and pillow.

Your general assessment of the children's efforts could, for instance, include an immediate appraisal of their oral communication skills. You take the chance to extend their vocabulary with such words as, 'stitch', 'sew', 'staples', 'stapler', 'stuffing', 'fold', and 'neat'. You make a mental note that the children might explain better if they demonstrated or 'modelled' what they wanted to do. For instance, they might fold materials to show what the final shape would look like. You also note that the children need to give more attention to 'stitching' the felt with more care to produce a more uniform finish. These will be things you will demonstrate and encourage in future tasks until the habit and skill are acquired. In the meantime, you give particular praise to those who did finish the products relatively neatly, signalling to the children that you value this. As the children worked on Teddy's bed problem, you took the opportunity to check that the children understood the problem and how their activities would solve it. You looked particularly for the ability to give reasons for their actions. During this, you found that one or two children could tell you what they planned to do next but left previous tasks unfinished. Was this because they did not know how to finish them? You sat with them and asked about their unfinished blankets. Had they simply forgotten about them? It was apparent that the attraction of the pillow-making task was too great for one child. She promised she would finish the blanket. Another reminded you he had been off when the others had used the 'funny' (pinking) scissors. You found some scraps of felt and had him practise with the pinking scissors. At the end, you mentally reviewed the class. You knew some had solved the problem successfully and used their new-found skills to good effect. You also felt that everyone had made worthwhile contributions, shown evidence of grasping the problem and of designing and making to solve it with success. Overall, you felt that the activities had achieved your goals and you had some pointers to what you needed to focus on in the future.

With older children, an appropriate task could be to have them design and make a hand garment for a really cold day. You want to use the task to develop a new skill when working with textiles, to give the children an opportunity to think creatively, to plan a sequence of actions, to consider appearance, to mark, cut out and join the materials with sufficient accuracy, and to evaluate the product.

Garments for hands present certain making problems so you have the children develop their knowledge using books and ICT resources. The questions they have to address are: Why do we have handwear? Can they sort handwear into three or four groups? What is the difference between muffs, mitts and gloves? What are the advantages of each? What are the disadvantages of each? What kinds of fabrics do people like best on cold days? What colours do they prefer? (They could do a class survey for the last two questions and present the results using ICT.) You read their written reports and find that they have handled this well. You now set the task: Design and make a better hand garment for a cold day. The children draw up a short list of desirables for the hand garment. You find you have to encourage certain children to be more adventurous and move away from standard mitts and gloves. You point out that the garment might do more than just keep hands warm. They sketch and develop ideas, mainly centred on variations of mitts (for example, mitts with Bulldog clips attached to hold bus tickets) and muffs (for example, with a central compartment to hold a radio). You collect these designs and review them. You see that some are imaginative, feasible and relate to the outcomes of the children's surveys. Others ignore the list of desirables and a few are impractical. You write appropriate advice on the children's work and allow time for revisions. The children are now ready to learn about making a pattern. You show them how to draw around an object and allow for a seam. You demonstrate this by cutting out a simple purse, sewing it and turning it inside out. The children make patterns for their hand garments and complete the task. You observe them as they work and feel reasonably satisfied with the care they take in marking out, cutting and sewing. You have them evaluate their designs for how well they achieved the desirables and for appearance. You read and mark these reports, looking for thoughts about product and process. Overall, you felt the task had achieved its ends for most of the children. You are, however, thinking about how you might use the next task to help some children be more innovative.

Assessing to inform others

Sooner or later, you will have to provide an account of each child's capability. Often, this is for the child's parents or carers and the next teacher. For instance, it is the practice to prepare an account of what each child can do as he or she approaches the end of the 3 – 5 stage. As these very young children are unlikely to learn D&T as a specific subject, this does not include an assessment of what the children can do in D&T. It does, however, draw on the children's performance in D&T-related activities. For instance, if the children make a fruit salad, you might reflect on their use of common implements. Similarly, if they make a ladybird, you might consider their shaping and assembling of materials. Your assessment is made by observing some aspects of a child's behaviour and matching it to given criteria. In assessing Physical Development, for example, the above tasks could provide evidence that a child has, 'fine motor control and co-ordination' or 'handles tools, objects, construction and malleable materials safely and with basic control', both indicators of physical development. A child need not perform at such levels every time but should show a tendency to do so. Your observations take into account those of parents and other adults.

In a similar way, teachers of older children may judge a child against statements of attainment written for those children. For example, by the time such children are approaching 11 years of age, they may be expected to 'generate ideas and plan what to do next', 'recognize what they have done well' and 'suggest things they could do better'. By the end of the stage, most should be able to 'make realistic plans', use 'words, labelled sketches and models to communicate', and 'use tools and equipment with some accuracy'.

It may seem that such 'Can Do' criteria will make assessment easy. This is not always the case. The first difficulty is that you need to interpret the criteria in terms of what are normal and reasonable expectations for the children concerned. It is expected that most children should 'use tools and equipment with some accuracy' as they approach 11 years of age. But what does this mean? There are very young children who can use scissors to cut along a line. Does this mean that they have achieved that level? The problem is that the context is missing. 'Some accuracy' means, 'with the accuracy reasonably expected of children in the tasks typical of what they do as they approach 11 years of age'. Being good with scissors is not enough.

Another difficulty with 'Can Do' lists is that they tend to break down D&T capability into isolated bits. A child may be able to do all the bits but that does not mean he or she can co-ordinate them. At the same time, tick lists may reflect a yes/no approach to assessment. This leaves no room for the reality of learning which may be 'usually', 'sometimes', 'rarely' or 'excellent', 'good', 'fairly good', 'satisfactory', 'weak', or anything in between. There is also a tendency to turn 'Can Do' lists into exercises that give rise to products for marking. Children's design ideas are drafted then re-written neatly for assessment. The marks given reflect neatness, spelling and careful colouring as much as the thinking behind the ideas.

How do you overcome these difficulties? First, develop a feel for what you might reasonably expect of the children by looking at the D&T work of more experienced teachers and ask for advice from your D&T co-ordinator or headteacher. If they and you are satisfied that your expectations are appropriate, you are in a position to attempt a summative assessment. Second, to assign levels of attainment to children, try beginning with the child's work instead of the criteria. Consider it as a whole, thinking about how the child responded to it in its early stages, when developing an idea, in bringing the idea to fruition, and in evaluating the product. Bearing in mind any support you gave, sort the children into groups according to their capability. Now think about why you placed one child in a higher group than another. Finally, look at the statements of attainment or criteria and grade the children accordingly. In the process, you may move children up or down. There is evidence that this approach can produce reliable assessments, especially if you assess a range of work to arrive at an overall level of attainment.

For example, suppose you have children at the end of the 5 – 7 stage. According to the assessment information, most are expected to be at a particular level at the end of the stage, say, Level 2. Suppose these children recently did the Potato Bag task in which they had to design and make a better bag to carry potatoes. Based on talk with the children, observation, and the various pieces of work produced, you were able to put them into three groups. On reflection, you saw that you were a little unfair. One was in the least capable group because his bag had failed but he had generated feasible ideas, developed one, told you why the bag had failed and what he would do differently next time. Accordingly, you adjusted the groups. This made you think about the most capable group. Their bags had worked well, most looked good and the written work was sound. But you recall how you had to support one child quite a lot in the development of the handle and the strengthening of the bottom of the bag. Others in that group had not needed help. You decide to move that child into the moderately capable group.

Now you turn to the descriptions for each level of attainment, beginning with Level 2. You find that the description fits most of your moderately capable and most capable group fairly well. They 'generate ideas and plan what to do next', they use simple 'models, pictures and words to describe their designs', and 'they recognize what they have done well' and can 'suggest things they could do better in the future' In this task, they showed that they could select appropriate materials from the range you put out. This is reinforced by their performance on other tasks using different kinds of materials and where the children also showed they could select appropriate tools and techniques. Of the Level 1, 2 and 3 descriptions, Level 2 is the best fit for most of these children. But for four of them you decide that Level 3 is a better fit. You also decide the Level 1 description is the best fit for two of the moderately capable group and all of the least capable group, although some of these might reach Level 2 soon. This gives you your first summative assessment. By itself, it is not sufficient and you need to do it again with other tasks to check your decisions.

If you have children at the end of the 7 – 11 stage, the assessment information will indicate that most will be expected to attain a higher level, such as Level 4. Suppose you told the children about 'The Problem with my Garage' and set it for them to solve. You helped the children clarify the problem and then they listed various design matters they would have to think about (for example, protection from impact, not scratching the car, possible effects of water). The children generated a variety of ideas and documented them for you. Many also showed an awareness of the potential user's viewpoint, particularly where there was the risk that a device would scratch the car. At this point, it was clear that they needed some fairly detailed information about car shapes and dimensions in order to take ideas further. The children located and downloaded this information from car salesroom websites. You noted those who tried to take into account the variation in car dimensions so that their designs would work with most of them. You also saw that most of them were trying out ideas with scraps of materials before finalizing their designs. You made a mental note of those who did not do this but would have benefited from it. The designs and plans of action were submitted to you and you examined them, providing constructive comments on each, and noted those needing further guidance. You observed the children making their devices and checked that they were using appropriate materials, tools and techniques and gave due regard to safety. You noted occasions when there was an unexpected difficulty and watched for coping strategies. At the end, you looked at the quality of the product, how well it worked, and the child's account.

Taking all this together, you placed the children into three groups according to capability. You then thought about what made the most capable group different to the moderately capable group and what distinguished the latter from the least capable group. You gave particular attention to the possibility that you may have been swayed unduly by the quality of the paper products and the devices themselves. You checked your notes to remind yourself of the thoughts and actions that were not evident in the products. As a result, you adjusted the groups a little.

As before, you now turn to the descriptions of each level of attainment, beginning with Level 4. This could be the best description of most of the children. They should, for instance, 'generate ideas by collecting and using information', 'take user's views into account and produce step-by-step plans', 'model' ideas when appropriate, work with accuracy and give attention to the 'quality of the finish and to function', 'reflect on their designs as they develop', and 'identify what worked well and what could be improved'. This task gave opportunities for a number of these to be evident. Some of those in your most capable group, however, may be better described by Level 5. Similarly, some of the least capable group may be working at Level 4 and some may be better described as at Level 3. But, of course, you should not expect one piece of work to provide you with a definitive assessment.

Finally, if there is a parallel class, you may find it helpful to ask the teacher to check a few of your assessments while you do the same for his or her assessments. This helps to ensure that there is some agreement about what constitutes a particular level.

Summary

Assessment in D&T can serve a number of purposes: informing you about your teaching and particular children's learning needs, giving feedback to children, informing others about learning in D&T, and adding to the account of the school's work. It usually involves an assessment of the level of attainment in the processes of D&T, evidence of which can be short lived. In assigning levels of attainment, one approach is to consider each child's activity as a whole, sorting the children into groups according to similarities in the quality of their work. After this, any formal criteria are applied. To make the process of assessment more reliable, you should assess each child's performance over a range of activities and not rely on the outcome of one assessment alone.

CHAPTER 10

Subject Leadership in D&T

Why have a leader for D&T?

Without a competent leader, a subject languishes. New ideas pass the school by and opportunities are missed. Teaching can become stale and lags behind developments and expectations. When governments have their attention elsewhere, other areas of learning risk neglect. With no one to speak for it, D&T is pushed to the end of the queue, funding dwindles and teaching time is reduced. Ensuring that D&T is in the care of someone who enjoys teaching it and sees its educational potential can make a big difference to the status of the subject in the eyes of other teachers, the children, the governors and the parents. Such a person should support and develop the teaching of D&T in the school.

Supporting the teaching of D&T

Day-to-day support maintains the quality of D&T teaching. This includes, for instance, helping a colleague devise a practical problem, informing the headteacher about stock needs, picking up that missing hacksaw from the staff room, and possibly arranging to have clay objects fired at the nearby secondary school. In other words, day-to-day support involves:

- advising others about D&T and the teaching of it;
- managing resources, overseeing storage, taking stock, checking equipment and replacing missing or faulty items;
- liaison on D&T-related matters with advisory teachers, teachers in other schools and the Local Education Authority officers.

Advising others

Teachers with confidence in teaching D&T are more likely to give it time, try out ideas, talk with children about D&T, and foster D&T capabilities. As subject leader, you should support and value that confidence – you may need to draw on it. But teachers' backgrounds and interests vary. Some are less confident and tend to be cautious, never really challenging the children's thinking and skills. These teachers may not be aware of how their feelings can affect their teaching and the attitudes of the children towards D&T. As a subject leader, you should support these teachers so that the quality of teaching and learning is raised. How might you do this?

First, you must recognize that these are colleagues and peers to be respected as such. Second, they, like you, are probably overworked. They are also likely to be subject leaders themselves and have their own problems to solve. What you do is more likely to be successful if it saves them time and effort and is neither patronising nor demeaning.

Suppose you know that a colleague is teaching some aspect of D&T next week. You could mention an idea you read about recently. You could talk about it and say you would be interested to know if it works, pointing out how well it suits next week's topic. Later, you could ask how things went and, perhaps, try to involve others in the discussion. On another occasion, you may be able to arrange some team teaching with your colleague to try out a new D&T topic. This helps you keep your hand in with another age group and, at the same time, models the kind of teaching you want to encourage. It works best with joint planning that makes it clear who does what. Remember that the main aim is for your colleague to practise new strategies and develop confidence. This is more likely if your colleague participates fully.

When colleagues see that you are willing to provide advice, they will begin to ask for your thoughts on the topics they teach. Thinking on the move may not be your *forte* but there is nothing wrong with having a source of ideas to hand to consult. You could use this book in that way and you might consult the QCA Scheme of Work (England) to see if there is anything there which would serve as a starting point. This saves time and gives an immediate response while the interest is there. Like other subjects, D&T teaching should also support cross-curricular aspects of learning, such as literacy, numeracy, personal, social and health education, problem-solving and creativity. Collect teaching ideas from professional journals about these aspects and talk about them with your colleagues.

For example, personal, social and health education aims to foster confidence, responsibility and an inclination to make the most of abilities. Amongst other things, it aims to have children develop healthy lifestyles and good relationships with others that respect differences between people. Elsewhere, the primary school is urged to develop problem-solving skills and foster creativity. What can D&T lessons do for these?

First, D&T lessons aim to develop practical problem-solving skills. This is a valuable life skill that can add to a child's confidence to engage with the world. Generating ideas and turning one into an effective product involves creativity. The writer, Arthur Koestler (1968), wrote that creativity involved the bringing together of two ideas to make a third and that is often what happens when we solve a practical problem. It also shows children that such problems often have more than one solution and these involve choice, economics and a weighing of benefits and disadvantages.

Second, amongst your D&T activities will be some that help you teach other aspects of personal, social and health education. For instance, matters of hygiene and healthy eating enter into food technology. Similarly, there are times when the children must collaborate successfully to solve a problem. This can be used to develop personal relationship skills and respect for others. By its nature, making a product often involves the safe use of tools. Attitudes of responsible behaviour can be fostered at such times. Some of the problems you set the children will be about helping those who cannot help themselves. For example, animals need shelter and the infirm may need a mechanical aid. Attending to such needs can foster an inclinaton to care about others. Care for the environment is involved in activities to do with the problem of litter in the playground, chewing gum on the steps, and tidiness in the classroom. At the same time, children see that a solution to a practical problem is sometimes of mixed benefit. The mobile phone, for instance, is both a boon and a bane.

Managing resources

D&T needs tools, materials, safety equipment, ICT and books. In some schools, these are stored in each classroom and are the responsibility of the class teacher. This allows D&T lessons to be taught in a flexible way. Opportunities can be taken as they arise and extended as needed. In other schools, tools and materials are held in a central store and issued as needed. This generally means teachers must stick to the allocated slot on the timetable or reserve particular items beforehand. Both systems can work but the second needs your direct supervision to make it effective. Have a clipboard in the cupboard that lists the contents so you can check them easily. Also check that things are safe to use. And, of course, remember that an unlocked tool cupboard may be just what after-school intruders want.

This sounds like having tools and materials in each classroom is the easier option. However, you still need to check them regularly to ensure they are safe to use. Keep a record of the date of checking and note any action taken. Tools should be locked away when not in use.

Liaison with others

Usually, a school needs a point-of-contact person for each aspect of its work. As the leader for D&T, information about courses, catalogues, requirements and developments should find their way to you. Be organized in the way you file these – someone may need them at short notice. You should also become known to your Local Education Authority's advisor or consultant responsible for D&T, if there is one. They can be a useful source of advice, particularly on rules and regulations. They may also offer training to support and develop D&T teaching. In due course, you are likely to make contact with secondary school D&T teachers. For instance, there may be a programme for smoothing the passage from primary to secondary school that involves meetings. You may be called upon to describe the D&T in Years 5 and 6. It can help to show photocopies of the children's work and pictures of their D&T products. In return, you will see what Years 7 and 8 do. This lets you and your secondary school colleagues ensure that the transition is relatively smooth. Do not, however, be tempted to adopt approaches that are better suited to the secondary school.

Like other subject leaders, you will have a significant role to play in preparing for the school's inspection. Inspectors expect to see paper 'evidence' of the school's provision in each area. Do not leave this task to the last minute. If you do, you may not have all the information to hand, it will be just your luck that the photocopier breaks down, and you will find the task very stressful. From the start, maintain a filing system that includes what inspectors generally want to see: copies of the school's policy referring to D&T, schemes of work, your assessment and recording system, and examples of children's work across the school. Also have to hand information on and examples of D&T's contribution to cross-curricular aspects of the school's work, such as literacy, numeracy, personal, social and health education, problem-solving, and creativity. Consider any recent initiatives relating to work in the primary school and make sure you have evidence of D&T's contribution to it, where relevant. Remember that inspection tends to be a mechanical exercise. Inspectors have lists of what to look for and may not have discretion in how they use them. For some things, paper evidence may be essential.

Meetings and training sessions relating to D&T need to be minuted or documented and copies kept as evidence. This can be tedious in a small school where much is done informally but, at the least, maintain a record of such 'meetings' in a book kept for that purpose. The outcome of an inspection may call for some action in the school's provision of D&T education. This involves development, the subject of the next section.

Developing the teaching of D&T

Developing the teaching of D&T is about identifying what needs to be done to improve D&T education in your school and to meet new requirements. People do not always take well to change – it usually means work and may involve something they are not good at. Understandably, people prefer to keep their deficiencies to themselves. In addition, when a lot is changing around you, more change is not likely to be welcome. Developing D&T involves:

- keeping informed about regional and national matters relating to D&T and disseminating information;

- preparing, updating and changing working documents;

- anticipating and responding to expectations and requirements.

Keeping informed and disseminating information

The least aggressive kind of change is when teaching evolves over time so that it is always more or less what is required. To achieve this, you must keep yourself informed. This is easier if you are a member of the primary school section of a professional body such as the Design and Technology Association (DATA). Otherwise, look for updates in professional journals, let your colleagues know that you are interested in such developments and ask them to draw your attention to relevant articles, courses and ideas. Think about what you read and hear. When attending a course, find out what is going on in other schools. Digest it and then bring it to your headteacher's attention.

Keep your colleagues informed about trends and new ideas. Do not burden them with speculation but prepare them for what will happen and give them time to accept the need. Try not to be the messenger of bad news. Not all changes are major and you will often pick up good ideas that your colleagues will welcome and can use now, in their classrooms. For instance, you may find that other schools have the children work with a wider range of materials than is normal in your school. You feel this would add to and improve D&T education in your school so you develop some ideas and, with the headteacher's permission, present them at a staff meeting. Make sure that the examples you show are directly relevant to your colleagues' work. If they can see that relevance and how it relates to their teaching, they are more likely to respond positively.

Dissemination extends to parents and governors. Parents' conceptions of subjects usually reflect their own school experiences but things may have moved on since then. How parents respond shapes what the children think. The danger is that children develop inappropriate conceptions of the subject and deny themselves opportunities for valuable learning, now and in later years. You could use the school newsletter to let parents and carers know about your school's D&T and have a display for adults to see when they visit. Use these to make the aims and value of D&T clear. Similarly, keep governors informed about developments and changes. You could, for instance, make a short presentation of examples of the children's work.

Preparing, updating and changing working documents

A school's policy statement describes what the school supports in its care and education of children. Policy statements are generally quite brief and that for D&T should be similar. It should state:

1. The nature of D&T.

2. Why D&T is taught in your school.

3. How D&T is taught in your school.

4. How D&T is managed in your school.

5. How it contributes to cross-curricular and other aspects of the children's education.

If you have to prepare a policy statement, Chapter 1 and your official documents for D&T will give you two or three sentences that describe the nature of D&T. For instance, you might begin, 'D&T is the solving of practical problems. In the primary school, it involves designing and making simple products from a variety of everyday materials using simple tools.'

In a similar way, you might supply reasons for teaching D&T in your school. For example, you might write, 'The teaching of D&T is a requirement of the National Curriculum. We value it because it develops important life skills (such as practical problem-solving capabilities) and fosters creativity and independence.' In addition, there may be something in your school's aims that allows you to add other reasons.

Regarding how the subject is taught in your school, you might write, 'The children develop their D&T capabilities (using knowledge and understanding to develop ideas, plan, communicate, work with tools and materials, and evaluate processes and products) in a variety of ways. While we favour learning by doing, we consolidate and develop this through other approaches, as when the children explore and discuss existing products.' You will, of course, include the approaches favoured by your school and will also need to relate these to the policy and strategies for ensuring the inclusion of all children.

The management of D&T refers to its short-term maintenance and its long-term development. You might begin, 'D&T education in the school, as with the rest of the curriculum, is the responsibility of the headteacher. He/she is advised by a subject leader/co-ordinator who oversees the daily maintenance and longer-term development of the subject.' You might continue by describing briefly who teaches D&T (for example, 'All class teachers teach D&T to their classes') and state the practice regarding access to materials and tools. You could conclude with your own responsibilities (for example, 'The subject leader is responsible for ...').

Finally, you would draw attention to what D&T can do for other aspects of the children's education. For example, you might mention, 'D&T can make a significant contribution to the development of children's problem-solving skills and provides opportunities for creativity. Similarly, it provides opportunities for developing social skills and respect for others' ideas. It also helps to make children safety conscious, not just for themselves, but for those around them. D&T provides many opportunities to practise and develop ICT skills and contributes to the development of numeracy and literacy. It can also be a major tool for integrating learning across the curriculum so that it makes learning more meaningful and durable.' Knowing your own school, you will have other things to add.

You must now ask yourself: To what extent is this policy being achieved? Are the children learning as much as they might? Are teachers making the most of D&T to achieve other aims of the curriculum? You will probably already have a feel for the answers to these questions and a lot can be learned from displays of the children's work in each classroom. Discuss and clarify your thoughts with the headteacher. The next step is to draw up an Action Plan. This may involve a revision of the school's scheme of work.

The school's scheme of work is what brings the policy to life. Draft an outline for discussion with your colleagues. Find out what each teacher enjoys and does well. Try to include these topics in the scheme so that the teachers feel comfortable with it. Nevertheless, in order to make the level of demand and quality of experience for the children appropriate in each year, you are likely to make changes and suggest activities. It can help to list more topics than are needed and let your colleagues choose which they will use. This gives them some control and makes change less uncomfortable. But remember that the headteacher has made you responsible for ensuring that the requirements of the National Curriculum are met. The scheme of work must reflect those requirements, at the least.

At times, the scheme of work may be satisfactory but the teaching has drifted away from it. You may need to bring this to colleagues' attention. When teaching becomes stale, it often helps to change what is taught rather than just urge people to do better. People become bored with doing the same thing, year after year. Injecting some new ideas may be just what is needed to refresh teaching.

Some tensions in your role

Although the subject leader's list of duties varies from school to school, it can be long and may include responsibilities that are not easy to fulfil. Reasons are often to do with a lack of resources, a lack of power and a lack of support.

For example, you may be 'in charge' of D&T but what does 'in charge' mean? Few have the power to order another teacher to do what they say. You may have made a great effort to arrive at a scheme of work by consultation and discussion but, if a teacher does not follow it, what can you do? You are usually very dependent on persuasion. First, be sure that there is not a good reason for failing to comply. If there is an acceptable reason, help the teacher solve the problem. Sometimes, drawing the reason out may not be easy. If, for instance, the teacher lacks the knowledge needed to teach what you expect, she or he may be reluctant to admit it and provide spurious reasons. In the event of a rare, bloody-minded refusal to comply, you need the help of someone who does have the power to insist. This usually means involving the headteacher. However, try everything else first because a discontented teacher may comply when observed but not otherwise. Participation in workshops and training sessions also calls for co-operation. A quiet, passive resistance can make them worthless for the teacher concerned (and embarrassing if you have brought in outside help; the headteacher may require attendance but it needs more than that). You should be sure that what you organize is seen positively by your colleagues. If the idea comes from them, all the better.

If you are expected to monitor and support individual teachers' D&T teaching, this can only be done during lesson time. You can only provide direct support if there are arrangements that make it possible. There is the potential for another tension here unless provision is made for you to be available. If you do not have some non-teaching time, this means someone must take your class occasionally. (If some-one takes your class for you, it can create a personal tension as you help others and 'neglect' your own class.)

A third tension can arise when you are routinely allocated insufficient funds to meet expectations. One problem is that you may not know what is needed before you agree to be the subject leader so it cannot be negotiated at the outset. You can, however, discuss the possibility of an initial sum to make good deficiencies followed by an annual sum for replacements and developments. As new requirements come along, you may have to return for additional, one-off funding.

A fourth tension can arise if you feel your own knowledge is inadequate. Perhaps you feel comfortable with the D&T you normally teach but now you are expected to advise others, take the lead in staff meetings and deliver workshops. Surely, your ignorance will show itself sooner or later. This is a tension you can resolve yourself. The first step is to avoid claiming to be an expert: some people enjoy seeing an expert discomfited. The second step is to read around the subject. This book provides much of what you need and you can refresh your D&T knowledge through books used by the children. The third step is to stick with it. Your knowledge and expertise will develop as you do the job. Attend courses, examine software as it arrives, look at catalogues and try out activities yourself. Remember that a steep learning curve will get you there sooner.

Summary

D&T can benefit from a guardian and a champion. On a day-to-day basis, the role involves helping others, managing tools and materials, and liaising with outside bodies. In the longer-term, it involves keeping yourself and others informed about developments, managing documentation and smoothing the way for change. Like many roles that involve responsibility without executive power, it can have its moments of tension. Some diplomacy, forethought and skills of persuasion combined with an attitude of respect for colleagues are likely to be useful attributes.

Further Reading

Chapter 1: What is Design and Technology?

There are lots of books about history and inventions that are informative and also potentially useful in the classroom, at least with older children. You might look out for: *James Dyson's History of Great Inventions* edited by R. Uhlig (2001) Constable, London. *A History of Invention* by T.I. Williams (1999) Macdonald, London. or *Key Moments in Science and Technology* by K. Wickes (1999) Hamlyn, Octopus, London. Those with a particular interest in the nature of technology education might look for *Issues in design and technology teaching* edited by S. Sayers, J. Morley and B. Barnes (2001) Routledge, London).

Chapter 2: Thoughtful Designing and Making

An interesting and readable book that describes research on D&T teaching in the primary school in a very accessible way is *Teaching and Learning Design and Technology* edited by J. Eggleston (2000) Continuum, London. For instance, it has chapters on curriculum development (Claire Benson), the interplay of designing and making skills as children practise them (Rob Johnsey), thoughts on problem-solving (Peter Taylor), and learning through making (John Eggleston).

Chapter 3: Teaching Designing and Making

An account of what children can do well and what they find difficult when solving problems is provided by P. McGhee (1997). 'Problem-solving within the age group 5 – 14', *School Science Review*, December, 79: pp. 103–10. The journal is available in many libraries. Those interested in creative thinking may like to read E. de Bono's *Parallel Thinking* (1994) Viking, London. Two publications which give important guidance on safety when teaching D&T are: Association for Science Education *Be Safe!* (2002) ASE, Hatfield and *Safety Guidelines for Key Stage 1 & 2: Design and Technology* (undated) TTS, Alfreton.

Chapters 4, 5 & 6: Some D&T-Related Activities for 3 – 5 years, Some D&T Activities for 5 – 7 years and for 7 – 11 years

See also the latest curriculum information specific to a given country. This can generally be accessed through government websites. For example:

England *www.hmso.gov.uk/guides.htm*
Northern Ireland *www.deni.gov.uk/teachers/curriculum/d_primary1.htm*
Scotland *www.scotland.gov.uk and www.LTScotland.com*
Wales *www.learning.wales.gov.uk* and
www.accac.org.uk/schoolcurric/School_curric_in_Wales/Intro.htm

For the 3 – 5 stage, I. McCleod-Brudenell's *The Design and Technology Handbook for Pre-School Providers* (1998) Design and Technology Association (DATA), Wellesbourne is a short book offering useful advice. There is also *Science and technology for the early years: purposeful play activities* by P. Allen (2002) Brilliant Publications, Dunstable.

For the 5 – 11 stages, particularly for those with an interest in using frameworks, there is David Jinks' *Professor Links and Tinkerton Tinx* (2000–3), one each for Structures and Mechanisms, and a Curriculum Guide and CD, with illustrations by S. Scurlock, Eduvision, Sheffield).

Chapter 7: Talking about D&T

A book that describes the invention of those simple things that we use every day and that are generally familiar to children is by J. Levy, *Really Useful: the origins of everyday things* (2002) Quintet Publishing Ltd., London. It provides the background which will help you talk with confidence about particular artefacts, like the safety pin, paper clip, and the eraser. It is not a book for children.

Chapter 8: Helping Children Make Progress in D&T

Planning, teaching and assessing the curriculum for pupils with learning difficulties: Design and Technology (2001) The Qualifications and Curriculum Authority (QCA), London, pp. 1–13, offers guidance and exemplification.

Chapter 9: Assessing D&T

A very clear and readable account of the introduction and development of Design and Technology in England and Wales and the difficulties of assessing D&T is by R. Kimbell, *Assessing Technology* (1997) Open University Press, Buckingham. It also describes D&T education in other countries.

Chapter 10: Subject Leadership in D&T

A book that describes the role of the subject co-ordinator in the primary school is by M. Briggs, *Your Role as Primary School Subject Co-ordinator* (1997) Open University/Hodder & Stoughton, London. Further information on many of the topics introduced in this chapter is available here.

Appendix

The following pages show some sheets that may support children in their thinking about various processes in design and technology. By their nature, worksheets are better suited to children who can read and write fairly well. You could use them as they are or adapt them to suit your needs or make them more specific to suit a particular task. You could also, of course, simply use them as examples and devise your own materials.

These pages are not meant to replace you and your talk with the children. They may help you give more time where it is needed but your personal interaction can be very important for the quality of learning. Nor are these pages meant to be ends in themselves – merely products for marking. They are to help the children design and make thoughtfully.

The final photocopiable pages are for you to use when planning activities. Step-by-step instructions are included.

Tell me about the story

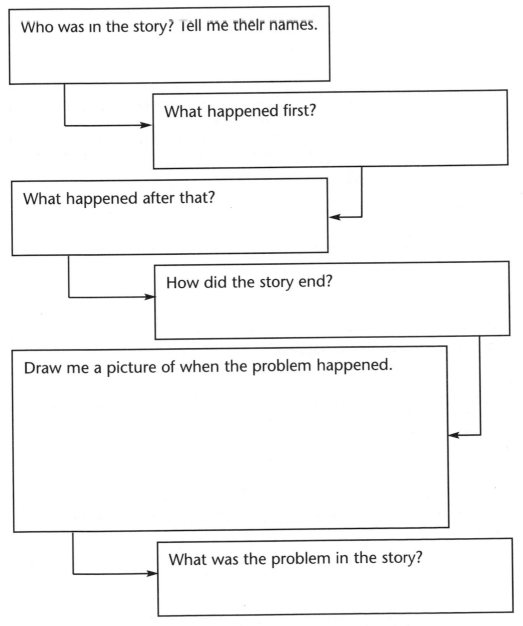

Who was in the story? Tell me their names.

What happened first?

What happened after that?

How did the story end?

Draw me a picture of when the problem happened.

What was the problem in the story?

Tell me about the problem

Draw me a picture to show me what the problem is.

Tell me in words what the problem is.

Where does this problem happen?

Why does this problem happen?

When does this problem happen?

If your idea solves the problem, how will you know you have solved it?

The 'How many ways?' game

This is a game for two people. The aim is to collect as many points as you can.

Step 1

Cut out the shape by cutting along the lines.
Fold the shape along the lines that are left to make a cube.
Fix the sides in place using adhesive tape.

Step 2

Decide who goes first by tossing a coin. The one who gets heads goes first.

Step 3

Each person throws the cube and answers the question that comes up on the top.
If they can do that, they get the points it says on those sides.
They put crosses on that side if they answer correctly.
Remember how many you score each time.

Step 4

Throw the cube again. If it comes up with a side on top that has a cross on it,
throw it again. You answer questions only on sides without crosses.

The winner is the one with most points.

		Why does the problem happen? 2 points	
What is the problem? 2 points	**What would you do about the problem?** 2 points	**What would you do about the the problem?** 2 points	**When does the problem happen?** 1 point
		What would you do about the problem? 2 points	

© 2005 Douglas Newton *Teaching Design and Technology 3–11*

What will I do?

What will you do about the problem?
Work out your ideas by drawing pictures here.
The pictures do not have to be perfect. You can change your mind.
This is your **thinking space.**

Now decide which idea you will start with.
The idea I will start with is:

----

because

Is there a part of your idea that you are not sure about?
If yes, what is it?

What will you do about that part? (Remember, you have the back of this
page to do some more thinking and drawing on.)

Sorting out my idea

Getting my thinking started

The idea I am going to use is

I am going to use this idea because

The easy-peasy bits

The parts I think will be easy will be:

I think this will be easy because

The hard bit

The part I think might be the hardest is

I think this might be the hardest because

What I am going to do about it is

(Draw a picture on the other side of this page if it helps you to explain what you will do or make.)

How I will make my idea

Show me with pictures how you will make your idea.

Draw a picture of what you will do first, here. **1**	When you do this step, put a tick on it.

Draw a picture of what you will do next, here. **2**	When you do this step, put a tick on it.

Draw a picture of what you will do next, here. **3**	When you do this step, put a tick on it.

Draw a picture of what you will do next, here. **4**	When you do this step, put a tick on it.

If you need more pictures, draw them on the other side of this page.

My Plan

Plan what you will do.
Begin with what you will do first and think of what you will do after that.
Be careful to get your plan in the right order. Write in pencil until you get it right.
Use your plan as you work.
When you finish a step, tick it in the box like this.

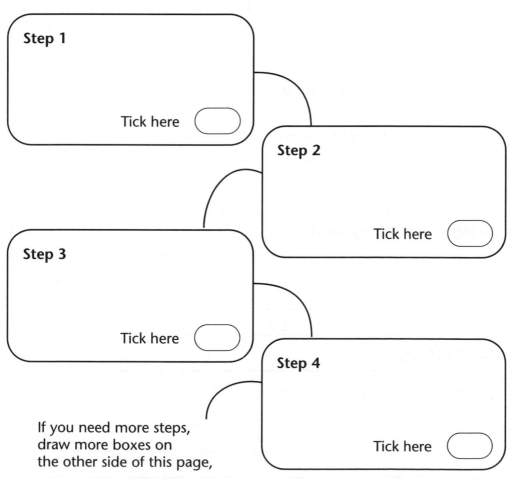

Step 1

Tick here

Step 2

Tick here

Step 3

Tick here

Step 4

If you need more steps,
draw more boxes on
the other side of this page,

Tick here

Getting ready

What will I need?

MATERIALS	TOOLS

What will I have to think about?

Being safe with my materials

Being safe with my tools

When I tidy up

I will make sure that

How did I do?

Think about what you have made and answer these questions.

1. Remind me what the problem was.

The problem was ---

----

2. How would you know if you had solved the problem?

I would know my idea solved the problem if it could do these things:

----

3. Did your idea do these things?

----

4. Is there something it does really well? What is it?

Why does it do that well?

----

5. Is there something it could do better? What is it?

Why did it not do that well?

How would you make it better if you were to do it again?

----

6. Did you forget about something? If yes, what was it?

Planning activities

The next photocopiable sheets provide a structure for your planning of practical activities. The first is to use when planning for 3 – 5 year olds. The second is to use when planning for 5 – 11 year olds. You may find it effective to proceed as follows:

Step 1: Decide what the learning opportunities/targets are to support progress. List these briefly in the box provided.

Step 2: Select or devise activities that will provide the learning opportunities (see, for instance, Chapters 4, 5 and 6). Note them in the *Activity* or *Focused activity* and *Designing and making activity* boxes. Think through each activity and consider carefully health and safety matters and ensure the well-being of the children and others at all times.

Step 3: Consider the prior experience and knowledge the children might draw on in the activity. Note this in the *Prior experience* or *Knowledge resource* box. Ask yourself if you need to remind the children of it or develop it prior to introducing them to the activities. You may be able to do this naturally in the context of other activities or another subject, such as science.

Step 4: Now think of interesting, motivating starting points or contexts for introducing or embedding the activities and note them under *Starting points* or *Contexts*.

Step 5: Next, ask yourself how you will bring together and round off the children's learning. Enter this in the box for the *Follow-up* or *Closing event*. If it involves practical work, ensure that health and safety matters are taken into account.

Step 6: Any ideas you have for related 'Talkabouts' to use later in a spare few minutes or as another lesson (see Chapter 7), note them in the box, *Talkabouts*. (These may appear in the *Follow-up* or *Closing event* boxes if you intend to use them immediately after the activities. Note that there may be times when they could be used to remind or develop experience, knowledge and know-how, so could introduce the topic.)

Planning: 3 – 5 years

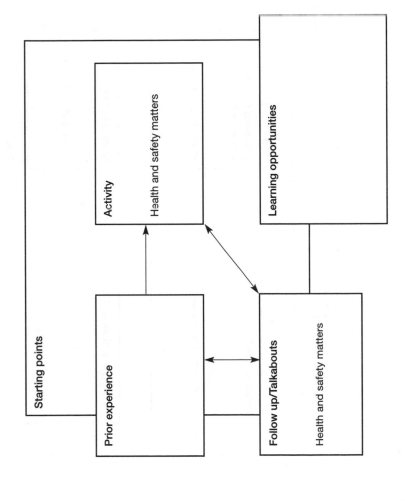

Starting points

Activity

Health and safety matters

Prior experience

Follow up/Talkabouts

Health and safety matters

Learning opportunities

Planning: 5 – 11 years

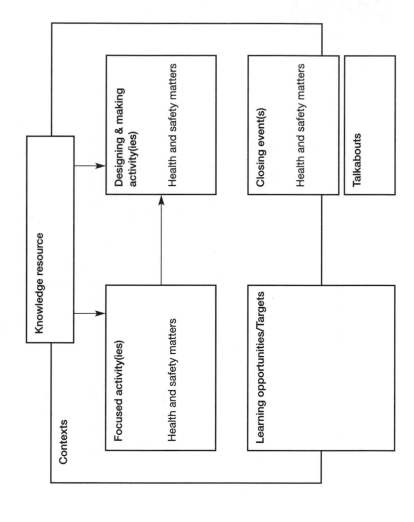

Bibliography

Awdry, W. (1946) *Thomas the Tank Engine*, Heinemann, London.

Davies, K. (1994) *Amelia Earhart flies around the World*, Zoe Books, Winchester.

DfES (2003) *National Primary Strategy: Excellence and Enjoyment*, DfES Publications, Annesley, Nottingham.

Carle, E. (1971) *The Very Hungry Caterpillar*, Hamish Hamilton, London.

Keillor, G. (1988) *Leaving Home*, Faber and Faber, London.

Koestler, A. (1968) *The Sleepwalkers*, Hutchinson, London.

Lindbergh, R. (1998) *Nobody Owns the Sky: The Story of Brave Bessie Coleman*, Walker Books, London.

Milne, A.A. (1999) *The House at Pooh Corner*, Egmont Chidren's Books, London.

Milne, A.A. (1999) 'A New House for Eeyore', in *The House at Pooh Corner*, Egmont Children's Books, London.

Nesbit, E. (1960) *The Railway Children*, Penguin, Harmondsworth.

Peppé, R. (1986) *The Mice and the Clockwork Bus*, Viking Kestrel, Harmondsworth.

Saxon, V. (1998) *Flik the Inventor*, Disney Enterprises, London.

Scarry, R. (1996) *Busytown Race Day*, Simon & Schuster/Aladdin, New York.

Index